Praise for **Joseph** ¶

T0151642

"Along with Joe Di Prisco, I rode that sa
But somehow, his was a local, with every stop an adventure: crime, passion, gambling, drugs, all the tantalizing stuff we goody-goodies missed."

— Leah Garchik, columnist, *San Francisco Chronicle*

"Joseph Di Prisco writes with humor and a great sense of character, poking fun at things that would leave a lesser author cringing. Think *Cuckoo's Nest* meets *The Godfather*. He interweaves all these elements with the skill of a master writer."

— Anne Hillerman, *New York Times* bestselling
author of *Spider Woman's Daughter*

"Great funny lines on every page. Am I recommending *The Alzhammer*? As the protagonist Mikey might say, 'Eggs ackly.'"

— Jack Handey, author of *Deep Thoughts*

"A brilliant portrayal of a wise guy who faces his biggest arch enemies... time and Alzheimer's. The last tango of power, fear, loyalty, and love is beautifully danced for us right to the very end."

— Vickie Sciacca, Lafayette Library

"A beautiful, heartfelt, sometimes funny, occasionally harrowing story of a man making his way through the minefield of his own family history. Di Prisco has lived more lives than most of us, and managed to get it all down in this riveting book."

— Jerry Stahl, author of *Permanent Midnight* and *OG Dad*

"Brimming with humor, heartbreak, and at times the feel an old-time Catholic confessional, *Subway to California* is a one-of-a-kind read."

— Kathleen Caldwell, A Great Good Place For Books

"A book replete with all the rich unfolding and poetic reflection of a novel, and all the focused research and unsparing truth-seeking of biography."
— Laura Cogan, Editor in Chief of *ZYZZYVA*

"What Di Prisco has written here is likely to become the standard-bearer for all future memoirs. This *Subway* ride is the real deal."
— Steven Gillis, author of *The Consequence of Skating*

"An attention-capturing cliffhanger."
— Judith M. Gallman, *Oakland Magazine*

"Told with enough tenderness and humor to elevate his pain-filled recollections to poetry at times, pure fun at others, Di Prisco brings us home — grateful our family is less volatile, or feeling less alone if we, too, survived a wild childhood."
— Lou Fancher, *Contra Costa Times*

"A heartwarming and hilarious sharing of his dysfunctional family adventures, Joe said it best when he wrote: 'Stories happen…to people who can tell them.'"
— Ginny Prior, *Oakland Tribune*

"A very fine novelist and poet who has now written a moving and actually quite funny memoir about life with two parents who should never have married, and once they did, should never have had children. But then we wouldn't have Joe to tell us their story."
— A. R. Taylor, author of *Sex, Rain, and Cold Fusion*

"People struggling to find their place in the world often search for answers in a psychiatrist's office, in love affairs, religion, illegal drugs, gambling, social activism, academia, work, and vicariously, through their children. Di Prisco visited all those places, and then, coming up short, found himself by writing a memoir."
— *Mercury News*

"It's rare to encounter a book so heartfelt and compassionate and yet so incisively hilarious at the same time."
— Heather Mackey, author of *Dreamwood*

"Throughout *Subway*, Di Prisco evokes the past with vivid, often hilarious, prose, describing his Italian-Polish upbringing in Brooklyn, the flight to a strange world called California, his doomed and dramatic love affairs, and his colorful parents—the kind of parents you enjoy reading about and are grateful they were not yours!"
— Anara Guard, author of *Remedies for Hunger*

"What makes Di Prisco's novel work is its narrative voice—poignant, rueful, and wise-crackingly sardonic...Readers of J. F. Powers' *Morte d'Urban* and Alice McDermott's *Charming Billy* should find their way to *All for Now*."
— P. F. Kluge, author of *A Call from Jersey* and *Gone Tomorrow*

"It is especially moving to read a book that looks so broadly at the ubiquitous issue of Roman Catholicism and pedophilia...Di Prisco has given us a brave, bumbling, soul-searching hero whose wry humor only enhances his honesty."
— Jan Weissmiller, Prairie Lights Books

"Catholic or not, religious or not, *All for Now* is accessible to everyone because mistakes and forgiveness are universal."
— *Seattle Post Intelligencer*

"*Confessions of Brother Eli* fairly sparkles with humor that ranges from sophisticated to slapstick, in what some believe to be the most difficult writing to carry off."
— *Tucson Weekly*

"With dry, sardonic wit, Brother Eli questions his faith and vocation, while recounting adventures that take place at his school…The writing and narrative voice in this book is some of the best I've come across."

—*Akron Beacon Journal*

"With a wit that questions as it embraces, *Poems in Which* provides us with a strong, original voice."

—Carl Dennis, author of *Practical Gods*
and winner of the Pulitzer Prize

COURT CLERK: Number 1 on the calendar, 1120 of '61, parole case, Joseph DiPrisco; Edward Potter, counsel.

MR. PATTEN: The People are ready for a disposition in that case, subject, of course, to your Honor's approval.

THE COURT: All right; proceed.

COURT CLERK: Joseph DiPrisco. Are you Joseph DiPrisco?

THE DEFENDANT: Yes.

COURT CLERK: Is Mr. Edward Potter your counsel?

THE DEFENDANT: Yes, sir.

THE COURT: Where's Mr. Potter?

MR. PATTEN: Your Honor, in view of the fact that the District Attorney is going to move for a dismissal of this indictment and Mr. Potter is not here, I think perhaps that we can proceed even in the absence of counsel.

THE COURT: Well, of course, that assumes that I am going to go along with the District Attorney. All right, I'll see that the defendant's rights are protected.

INDICTMENT No. 1120-61

State of New York }
County of Queens } ss.:

In the Name of the People of the State of New York

TO ANY PEACE OFFICER IN THIS STATE:

An indictment having been found on the **19th** day of **July, 1961**

in the **COUNTY** Court of the County of Queens, charging

JOSEPH DI PRISCO

with the crime of **Forgery 2nd Degree (6 Counts), Grand Larceny**

2nd Degree (4 Counts), Attempted Grand Larceny 2nd Degree

Conspiracy as a Misdemeanor

You are therefore Commanded forthwith to arrest the above-named

JOSEPH DI PRISCO

and bring **him** before that Court to answer the indictment, or if the Court have adjourned

for the term, that you deliver him into custody of the Warden, City Prison, in and for the County of

Queens, N. Y.

Dated at Long Island City, Queens County, the **19th** day of **July**, 19 **61**

Frank D. O'Connor

District Attorney.

The
Pope of
Brooklyn

Brothers: Joe and John Di Prisco. Berkeley, California circa 1965.

The Pope of Brooklyn

Joseph Di Prisco

A GENUINE VIREO BOOK | RARE BIRD BOOKS

Los Angeles, Calif.

A Vireo Book | Rare Bird Books
453 South Spring Street, Suite 302
Los Angeles, CA 90013
rarebirdbooks.com

Copyright © 2017 by Joseph Di Prisco

FIRST PAPERBACK EDITION

Set in Minion
Printed in the United States

10 9 8 7 6 5 4 3 2 1

Publisher's Cataloging-in-Publication data

Names: Di Prisco, Joseph, 1950-, author.
Title: The Pope of Brooklyn / Joseph Di Prisco.
Description: Includes bibliographical references. | A Genuine Vireo Book
First Paperback Edition | New York, NY; Los Angeles, CA:
Vireo Books, Rare Bird Books, 2017.
Identifiers: ISBN 9781947856608
Subjects: LCSH Di Prisco, Giuseppe Luigi. | Police corruption—New York (State)—
New York. | Criminals—New York (State)—New York—Biography. | Informers—
New York (State)—New York—Biography. | Organized crime—New York (State)—
New York—History—20th century. | BISAC BIOGRAPHY & AUTOBIOGRAPHY /
Criminals & Outlaws
Classification: LCC HV6248 D52 .D5 2017 | DDC 364.1/323—dc23.

To Patti

&

To friends relieved not to be mentioned

You came from Greenpoint. Go back to Greenpoint!

—*On the Waterfront* (1954)

We all have reasons

for moving.

I move

to keep things whole.

—Mark Strand, "Keeping Things Whole"

NAME: JOSEPH DI PRISCO   B # 496476

ALIAS: SHORTS   E #

This certifies that the finger impressions of the above named person have been compared and the following is a true copy of the records of this bureau.

D.C.I. # 888382X

F.B.I. # 954782D

Date of Arrest	NAME	Borough or City	CHARGE	Arresting Officer	Date, Disposition, Judge and Court
12-5-49	Joseph Di Prisco	Bklyn	Runner for Gambler	Reiter AHS D&R	12-21-49 Spec. Sess Crt. #7146
9-29-61	Joseph Di Prisco	Queens	Forgery 2nd & Gr. Larc.	Stone PCC10	
10-4-61	Joseph Di Prisco	Bklyn	Forgery (Warrant)	Schmidt BK Duo	

Record prepared on OCT 1 1961
Date

by _Vera McMillian_
Signature

Civ. Typist   BCI
Rank   Shield No.   Command

Arthur L. Morgan

Deputy Inspector

Bureau Criminal Identification

CONTENTS

Conspiracies of the Past

Fishing around on an ordinary online expedition, I landed more than I was looking for. I hooked a long-lost key to my life.

Alongside clickbait, listicles, celebrity trolls, and pestering pop-ups, the Internet does sometimes dish. Even so, I did not see this one coming. There was my name in bold face on the computer monitor, but it seemed to be mysteriously associated with fifty-year-old court records. How could I resist clicking on the links? Soon I realized these documents had nothing to do with me— but they had everything to do with me. These were transcripts of trials, and the star witness was a man who shared my first and last name, my father.

As I would come to learn, I had just discovered evidence of his untold, suspenseful life. The door into the past, which I assumed was sealed shut, was now unlocked. I was jolted. His testimony in these New York State Appellate Division proceedings spun a revealing and troubling tale, one that would resonate for generations in my family.

Technically, these were New York City police departmental hearings, with witnesses under oath, pertaining to the nefarious activities of dirty cops and his collaboration in their conspiracies. The trials, safe to say, have gone unnoticed and unremarked upon for over half a century. In the annals of American jurisprudence, then, not exactly O. J. or the Rosenbergs. In the annals of American me, different story. This was my old man, and the uncovered transcripts divulged an unobstructed, unfiltered glimpse. Who exactly was this enigmatic man? Did I ever know him? I now had some clues.

GIUSEPPE LUIGI DI PRISCO took the stand during that fraught epoch, the sixties, when the NYPD was generating frequent, embarrassing headlines as to corruption within the ranks. Buried in the court documents it is mentioned that the grand jury did not hand up charges against two of the cops he testified against; he was evidently considered unworthy of belief with regard to them. Those grand jury proceedings remain inaccessible, so there is no way to analyze the merits of their disposition. Meanwhile, three other police officers were drummed out of the force fairly totally on the basis of his testimony, or arrested, deemed culpable of committing shakedowns, and one of them ended up serving serious time on a related matter (extortion; burglary ring) that surfaced under questioning. My father's unexpectedly available online testimony related to a handful of such crimes, but it seems naïve to assume that these officers' reign of intimidation was restricted to that extent. It seems equally naïve to assume he wasn't aware of, and didn't play a role in, similar escapades he was not questioned about.

Informant may constitute an ignoble and perilous career option in the estimation of the genteel and the upright along with the incarcerated and the indicted, especially when the informant's burden entailed, as it did for my dad, ratting out people he knew and borrowed money from to gamble, or to pay off loan shark obligations. Snitches do get stitches. If nobody would consider him a caped crusader for justice, the cops he did business with were definitely not choir boys, and neither were the bookmakers and gamblers with whom he consorted.

Although police misconduct and abuse of authority and criminality have recently been in the glare of the national spotlight, it was also in the sixties when the reputation of the mighty Blue Line cratered. It would not be long before the Federal Bureau of Investigation infiltrated the compromised New York Police Department, the Internal Affairs Bureau would be established, and the City would empower the vaunted Knapp Commission. That panel was dedicated to the restoration of the traumatized public's confidence in law enforcement. To that end, personnel shake-ups and numerous arrests ensued.

That's when Frank Serpico became a household name, the subject of a best-selling book and a wildly popular, critically acclaimed movie. In the eyes of the City, if most certainly not in the view of all his fellow officers, he heroically embodied the zeal to clean up the force: a brave, whistle-blowing cop who risked his life and paid a high personal price for exposing police sleaze and machination. When Serpico was working Narcotics and they were moving in on an arrest, he was shot in the head by a drug dealer. Chances were he may have been set up—by the other cops. As he lay in a pool of his own blood, his backups did nothing, did not radio "Officer down," didn't call for an ambulance, though a bystander did and thereby saved his life. Afterward cop message boards contained sentiments along lines that were anything but sympathetic. "If it wasn't for that fucking Serpico," a precinct captain later said, he "could have been a millionaire." One police chief Serpico singled out as a "good guy" was Sidney Cooper. That's a name that pops up in the unearthed transcripts, in support of my father. As for the Serpico shooting, it took place about a mile from where I grew up.

Years before Knapp was created, there was its forerunner: the Police Commissioner's Confidential Investigations Unit. In 1961, as these trial transcripts dramatize, the PCCIU took up residence in my father's boxers.

New York State Appellate Division

RECORDS AND BRIEFS

Q. Would you say, Mr. Di Prisco, that before April 18th, 1961, you were known among your friends as a big criminal?

A. No.

Q. Were you known as a little criminal?

A. No, sir.

Q. Were you known as any kind of criminal, big, little, middle, were you?

A. No, sir.

Q. You didn't go bragging, or boasting, "I'm a criminal," to people, did you?

A. No, sir.

Q. Did you ever [say] that you were a racketeer of some kind, did you?

A. I'm not a racketeer.

Q. You never were, were you?

A. No.

Joseph DiPrisco, for Department, Direct

By Mr. McDonough:

Q. Mr. DiPrisco, have you ever been convicted of a crime?

> Mr. Herwitz: I object, if your Honor please, on the ground that the—whatever the conviction; this man may have had convictions—this man may have had, are not binding on the accused, Celentano.
>
> Dep. Com. Reisman: I assume, in the course of testimony, some effort will be made to connect it, and we must proceed in an orderly manner, on a sufficient basis.
>
> Mr. Herwitz: Do I understand, if your Honor please, this evidence is taken, to that obvious connection?
>
> Dep. Com. Reisman: Yes.

Q. And what crime? A. Bookmaking.

Q. And when were you convicted? A. 1949.

Q. Now, have you ever acted in the capacity as Informer for police officers? A. Yes, sir.

Q. And what would that work—

> Mr. Herwitz: Now, if your Honor please, I object on the ground that this is entirely irrelevant and immaterial, with respect to the first count of this—these charges.
>
> Dep. Com. Reisman: I'll take it with that understanding. Overruled.

Q. Now, what would that work consist of?

> Mr. Herwitz: I object, if your Honor please.
>
> Dep. Com. Reisman: Restate the question.

Q. What did the work entail? A. Turning up bookmakers.

> Mr. Herwitz: I object, and move to strike it out as irrelevant.

It Was True at the Time

When I was an altar boy in Brooklyn, priests and nuns taught us that the smoldering incense symbolized prayers lifting up to God. Me, I wasn't sold. Usually I felt lightheaded from inhaling the sweet reek of curling smoke. Such wooziness often washed over me during the late fifties and early sixties, about the same time my father was a young man on the hustle. On the street, Joe Di Prisco was called "Pope."

Clad in black cassock and bleached, starched white surplice, I was occupied lighting candles, genuflecting, tolling Sanctus bells. When the Mass celebrant intoned "Dominus vobiscum," *The Lord be with you*, I'd reply as instructed, "Et cum spiritu tuo," *And with your spirit.* My spirit and I had not yet acquired the inside information that my dad was a confidential police informant, petty criminal, scam artist, and stool pigeon. I was also unaware that felony indictments of his own would soon be hanging over his head. I never had an inkling he was discredited in open court as an "unsavory character" and a "known gambler"—which was the considered judgment of one presiding eminence. This was someone who added on the record, perhaps surprisingly, that he *believed* his testimony.

As a five- or ten-year-old, I myself hadn't yet been christened with a street name of my own, unless Jo Jo qualified; that was the theoretically cute handle my family used for me but it made me cringe. Around our claustrophobic Humboldt Street shotgun walk-up in Greenpoint my dad wasn't called Pope, and he wasn't smeared with the "unsavory character" label. There he was better known as an "Italian barbarian" and a "fucking antisocial degenerate." At least those were the terms of endearment screamed by his wife, my mother, in a voice to rattle the kitchenware.

Whenever I asked her, my mother with a trucker's mouth, why they called him Pope, her stock answer was "Because he never shuts the fuck up." That made no sense to me, but his own explanation of his name's origins was more puzzling: once his crew observed him coming out of a church. This sounded peculiar if not dubious to me, because I myself had very sparse memories of his being inside a church and therefore could not visualize him stealing inside to light a votive candle or make confession.

Growing up and working the angles in the day: when I look back, I imagine such vocation might sound entrancing if not inevitable to somebody like my father. Ample evidence demonstrates that the calling resonated for him—much as it might do later on, in complicated, indirect ways, for me and my younger brother.

～

IN ONE LEGAL PROCEEDING he testified against plainclothes police officers in 1961 on charges stemming from a shakedown four years earlier. The crime's execution was somewhat convoluted, as with a lot of capers, though it wouldn't ever be confused with *Ocean's 11* or *The Sting*. My dad was thirty-two the day he and the cops conspired to set up a bookmaker by the name of Sal Valenti for the purposes of squeezing some cash out of him.

On the street they accost Valenti, whom my father zeroed in on, and tell him to get in the car. The guy naturally fears for his life. He's probably seen the movies, or maybe he has a three-digit IQ and he's asking himself if obeying strangers instructing you to get in their car ever worked out well in Brooklyn or any other borough. Once the book is ushered into the backseat, he hears his options: door number one, the cops arrest him with those incriminating betting slips in his possession and run him in, which—if he was following the bouncing ball—would damage his enterprise and lead to fines and imprisonment; or door number two, the man ponies up cash and the whole thing never happened. The way the bookmaker should look at it, this could be his lucky day. That's when they squire Valenti home and seize six hundred bucks, a lot of money in 1961, and later—what arrest?

During that and every other trial, counsel for the cops' defense relentlessly grilled my dad, who admitted fingering unfortunate bookmakers for the accused policemen to score. The fancy suit whittled away at Pope's trustworthiness. It's reasonable to assume this strategy must have appealed to him as much as shooting fish in a barrel. In one hearing, he harped upon an apparent inconsistency in his previous testimony, and the two conducted a tortuous, heated exchange, which featured this dispositive moment:

> *Q. Do you remember being asked those questions and making those answers?*
> *A. Yes.*
> *Q. Was that answer true?*
> *A. It was true at the time.*

~

HIS LIE HAD BEEN true at the time.

Ladies and gentlemen of the jury, meet my old man.

As for the substance of his Pope-splaining declaration: Disingenuous? Evasive? Tactically ingenious? Epistemologically ridiculous? Cognitively sophisticated? Any chance factual or possibly honest?

I'm going with *All of the Above*, and if you knew my dad—my unmanageable, impulsive, bottled-up, unhinged, sentimental, take-no-bullshit, shifty, tough, smarter-than-he-wanted-you-to-think, dumber-than-you-could-believe, hyperactive, attention-deficit old man, a rakishly handsome guy of supposedly few words whom my *va va va voom* mother excoriated as somebody who, and I quote, "never shut the fuck up"—so might you. Then again, I am not convinced anybody could take an oath that they really knew him—including me, himself, his immediate and extended family, as well as any and all representatives of law enforcement. My whole life I tried to pin him down and I usually failed. At the same time, like a winter cold, he was tough to shake off.

～

CONVERSATION IN THE CITY with a New Yorker, asked if he grew up here.

"No," he said, and pointed, "one block over."

The Brooklyn where both my father and I grew up has little in common with the chichi Brooklyn of today. Nowadays Brooklyn is the home of cool television shows and movies, the home of the splashy Barclays Center, where Jay Z and Beyoncé and Spike Lee sit courtside for NBA games, the home of trendy restaurants that serve something other than the veal parm or pierogi that once used to dominate every menu, the home of a murderers' row of authors, and base camp of hipsters sporting stingy brims, man buns, Civil War beards, hoodies, e-cigs, and designer sneaks.

Wait, let me make an act of contrition. I think it's now against the law to use *Brooklyn* and *hipster* in the same sentence—or lifetime. So nobody should say that anymore. You utter the word "hipster" and everybody knows you're an idiot or, in other words, you probably come from California, where all you talk about is organic this and vegan that, the drought, the death of lawns, which—well, who cares about dumb lawns anyway? As for Brooklyn: nobody goes there anymore, it's too popular. Sue me, Yogi Berra's Estate. I miss Yogi, though not as much as my dad.

My father didn't exactly come out of nowhere, but it was close. It was on the mean streets of Brooklyn in the hardscrabble fifties where he made his bones. That was when and where the Dodgers of Ebbets Field, the legendary Boys of Summer, ruled the borough and therefore the world and, depending on who you were or even more who you were not, the wise guys and the wannabes called the shots.

New York State Appellate Division

RECORDS AND BRIEFS

Q. *Sergeant, I am going to show you a photograph of an individual. I want you to look at it carefully and state whether or not you have seen this person before. For the record Sergeant Ficalora has been shown a photograph of Joseph Di Prisco, B Number 18308, taken 9/26/61, in Berkeley, California. Sergeant, have you seen that photograph?*

A. *Yes.*

Q. *Have you had occasion to see the individual whose photograph I showed you?*

A. *Yes, sir.*

Q. *When was that?*

A. *At the DA's office in Queens on—that was Monday I guess, October 23rd.*

Q. *Have you ever seen that individual before?*

A. *Before then? No, sir.*

Q. *Have you ever heard of anyone referred to as Little John, Joe Shots, Joe the Pope or Mopey?*

A. *No, sir, not that I can remember.*

…

Q. *Did you ever hear the name Joe Di Prisco from your partner?*

A. *No, not until this all happened.*

Q. *Patrolman Tartarian never mentioned the name Joe Di Prisco to you?*

A. *No, sir.*

Q. *Did you ever have occasion to meet your partner and another man at Queens Plaza during the month of February, whereupon this man stayed in the car with you and your partner and made observations around*

Macy's Warehouse?

A. *No, sir.*

Q. *Do you know Sal Valenti?*

A. *Sal Valenti?*

Q. *Valenti, an employee of Macy's?*

A. *No.*

Down and Out in Brooklyn

Even a clueless little pain in the ass grudgingly responding to Jo Jo couldn't miss that something cataclysmic was up when we skipped out of Brooklyn. Our hasty, furtive exile took place under cover of night and ultimately deposited us on the opposite coast in the summer of 1961, a life-changing period for the Di Priscos.

The abrupt departure happened the day when—what-to-my-wondering-ten-year-old eyes—the old man did disappear. He and I and my little brother had been walking down a Long Island country road on a beautiful Sunday afternoon and then, in a flash, he hightailed it into the woods that swallowed him up. Left standing on the road, I needed only a moment to conclude he was fleeing the long arms of the law. Plainclothes and uniformed officers had descended in force, lights flashing on their patrol car roofs, that late spring or early summer day, throwing a net around his parents'—my Italian immigrant grandparents'—farm in East Islip, a net he slipped that day. I loved that farm, because what city kid doesn't love a farm with pigs and donkeys and chickens and rabbits and watermelons and tomatoes and corn, where Sunday suppers were feasts of *abbondanza,* but hold on a minute. Where the hell was he running, and why? It would take a while to find out where he thought he was going and much longer to understand why, not to mention how it related to me.

INDICTMENTS WOULD BE HANDED up on him that summer, and they eventually spurred his return to New York to testify against those cops—in an effort to avoid his own prosecution. Before that could happen, in the immediate term, and probably nothing's more immediate than being on the run from law enforcement, he ended up *anywhere* but Brooklyn, which is another way to identify the *California* where his road trip thudded to a halt at the Pacific's edge.

That was the summer, while he was in the wind, detectives were knocking on our Greenpoint door looking for him. I can still see how my older brother, Eddie, smirked as he greeted them standing out in the hallway, not inviting them in for high tea, defiantly announcing to my mother in the next room: "It's nobody, John Law." Then they stopped appearing. And then surveillance outside our apartment ceased, and the guys who had been camped out in the unmarked car on Humboldt Street evaporated.

Our street had been named for the founder of geophysics, Alexander Humboldt, nineteenth-century German explorer of the Orinoco and Amazon. Law enforcement disappearance probably provided the opening for my mother to put me and my brother John alongside her on a plane so we could do our own explorations in California, leaving behind her two older sons from a previous marriage, Bobby and Eddie, ages sixteen and seventeen, to fend for themselves in Brooklyn.

San Francisco was where we had our rendezvous with my dad, three thousand miles from home. He didn't greet us inside the airport terminal. He and his wife had worked out logistics. We took a taxi to a gas station, where we found him keeping a low profile, not daring to get out of his old black Ford with black New York plates, frozen fretful behind the wheel. Next thing I knew, we hit the road, going—God knows where.

The bottom line—or at least one of several bottom lines: my younger brother and I were shanghaied at eight and ten years old. Some think "shanghaied" isn't quite PC, but I can't see how the image implies an ethnic stereotype, and besides, when I was a little boy I wasn't finished with politically incorrect Brooklyn, and California existed in my mind as nothing more than a sun-drenched movie set. I was offered no explanation for being uprooted, for abandoning my friends without a word of warning and leaving my home for what I presumed would be the longest goodbye. Young children implicitly assume their fate is in the hands of their parents, for good or ill, but this move amounted to a seismic shift.

From the jump, I instinctively and righteously hated California, let me count the ways. Where do you get an egg cream, a knish? Where can you find a real bagel or a good deli or a decent slice? Because what they called bialy and a sub and pizza definitely did not qualify. Where were the stoops and the fire hydrant showers and the stick ball games? Where was the snow? More than anything else, where were my buddies? Here I was feeling isolated, a displaced little pious boy from Greenpoint. My ground was rocked, and I found myself in a state where the earth itself trembled what felt like continually, tectonically as well as psychologically. I wanted to trust my parents, naturally, but whatever was going on in my family was shrouded in shadows. It's taken me over fifty years to shed some light.

∽

BACK IN THE DAY, back before I was conscious that there was a historical day back before, I had no glimmering as to his criminal life, and I was unaware of those legal proceedings in which he was the witness for the People; they came to light for me more than two years after he died in hospice care at eighty-six from complications due to Alzheimer's and congestive heart failure, and less than a year after I published *Subway to California*, my first memoir. What also came to light was his criminal record in Brooklyn and Queens—by which I mean his criminal record did *not* come to light. Mysteriously, though, his trial transcripts were accessible online; fifty-some years later his files remained sealed in New York City. Why? And what could I do about unsealing them? It was destined not to be a simple task. When it came to my relationship with my father, nothing was ever without complication.

All this will take some explaining, and because I'm the last one standing, here goes.

⌇

SINCE THIS ISN'T MY father's book, or my mother's or little brother's for that matter, some questions continue to emerge for me.

Questions about fathers and their sons. About brothers and their father. As was the case when I was a little boy, I have nothing but questions.

Families sometimes appear bound together by the stories others weave about them as well as by the stories they spin themselves— when, that is, they aren't torn apart. Stories may also be held together by families, even after the narrative threads fray. Another way to put this is that families are myth-making organisms. They inevitably construct the sometimes wordless tales that illuminate the ordinary experiences of everyday life, as well as the tumult and the crises. How did somebody like me, the obsessive-compulsive schoolboy, go about fashioning the sustaining myth when the unknown is central—unless, that is, the unknown is itself the generative myth?

I wonder if I can ever with absolute assurance trace the arc of my father's life. Of course, human beings can change, in theory. Experience might harden one, experience might soften another, experience might lead others to hard-won wisdom. Some people apparently learn their most powerful cautionary lessons at their peril. Did my father harbor regrets, did he make amends, and once in California—assuming conventional values ever appealed to him, which is itself a big question—did he straighten up and fly right?

I could reply, probably so, or maybe sort of, but the reality is far more nuanced than that. If this is a tale of redemption, either his or mine, I might be the last to know. If my father heard such an accusation, my guess is he would change the subject or recommend I shut the fuck up.

Furthermore, what effect did his criminal life have upon his family? In particular, what was the impact upon his two sons? Mercifully, fewer people these days seem to reference the once popular notion of role modeling. To me, it's right up there on the clang-o-meter with *closure* and *self-esteem* building. Closure strikes me as being a bitter illusion as it relates to genuine tragedy; closure is to loss as intimacy is to pornography. And you know who enjoys self-esteem off the charts?

Death-row inmates and gangbangers. And you know who just might have abysmal self-esteem? Artists.

I'm not dreaming a closure dream and my own self-esteem has often been a horse running boxed-in on the rail and finishing out of the money.

In any case, role modeling never failed to strike me as being anything but reductive. Since when is a child's behavior the function of another person's? How does somebody else's inclination to angelic or demonic behavior control for the conduct and the choices of anybody else?

But maybe not so fast. Are criminal temperaments or, for that matter, artistic temperaments in some sense heritable? Evidence seems at a minimum mixed, if not dubious. The human beings I meet while boarding a plane or on the freeway or in a restaurant or at a party or during Mass or in my classes seem, to state the obvious, pretty complicated, virtually unpredictable. Artists and criminals are hardly mutually exclusive categories; there exist avant-garde criminals and outlaw artists. That said, if you conduct research in libraries or on the Web for something like "heritability and sociopathic tendencies," many, many books and longitudinal studies pop up, some suggesting the existence of some order of ingrained predisposition. Yet predisposition does not necessarily constitute destiny.

Nonetheless, despite not being a cognitive scientist like Stephen Pinker, because nobody else is, I would ask this, specifically: did my father's sons eventually come to follow, perhaps unconsciously, perhaps provisionally or experimentally, his career path? You may not be able to yet, but you will eventually see why I ask.

Here's a heads up: my answer is a definite yes, no, and maybe.

To phrase this more generally: what do we know about a father by knowing his sons? And then: what do we know about his sons, and their relationship with each other, by knowing about their father? At various stages in my own life, I might have answered both those questions about me and my lineage in the same way: we know absolutely *nothing*. At other points: we know *everything*. Nowadays, I am going with: we may indeed know *something*, but what is it?

I find Andrew Solomon instructive and chastening on this matter. He is the author of the magisterial *Far From the Tree: Parents, Children, and the Search for Identity*:

> Our children are not us: they carry throwback genes and recessive traits and are subject right from the start to environmental stimuli beyond our control. And yet we are our children; the reality of being a parent never leaves those who have braved the metamorphosis... Insofar as our children resemble us, they are our most precious

admirers, and insofar as they differ, they can be our most vehement detractors…

Because of the transmission of identity from one generation to the next, most children will share at least some traits with their parents. These are *vertical* identities. Attributes and values are passed down from parent to child across the generations not only through strands of DNA, but also through shared cultural norms…

Often, however, someone has an inherent or acquired trait that is foreign to his or her parents and must therefore acquire identity from a peer group. This is a *horizontal* identity. Such horizontal identities may reflect recessive genes, random mutations, prenatal influences, or values and preferences that a child does not share with his progenitors… Physical disability tends to be horizontal, as does genius. Psychopathy, too, is often horizontal; most criminals are not raised by mobsters and must invent their own treachery…

⌒

DECADES AGO I WAS a curious little boy who didn't know what the old man did all day, or if he kept a job, or where he went when he shambled out of our shotgun Greenpoint apartment and shuffled down the flights of stairs and onto the street or hopped into a car that sped off. When I found occasion as a child to ask him my incessant questions, his invariable response was:

Whaddayou, writin' a book?

Those were the days. A pillar of the Brooklyn ethos: never answer a direct question from a cop—or from a wife or a son. Gun to your ribs, respond with another question, ideally some wiseass variation on *Who wantsta know?* Nobody needed to know what nobody needed to know, get it? It's logical to deduce the old man had not consulted helpful parenting guides encouraging and cultivating the natural curiosity in that precious wonderland known as childhood. Except for Dr. Spock's, I don't think there were many popular parenting books circulating for the edification of the Greatest Generation. They certainly weren't trending in our home. Come to think of it, we didn't have any of those exotic objects lying around, *books*.

New York State Appellate Division

RECORDS AND BRIEFS

Q. *Now, Mr. Di Prisco, do you have any aliases, any nickname?*

A. *Yes, sir.*

Q. *What is it?*

A. *Pop.*

Q. *Pope? Or Pop?*

A. *P-o-p-e.*

Q. *Have you ever had any other nickname?*

A. *Well, I don't know, some—maybe somebody called me "Shots," but I—that is my nickname as Pope, that is the only one I know.*

Q. *I'm not asking you whether anybody called you "Shots." Did anybody call you "Shots" that you remember?*

A. *Not that I know of.*

Q. *In other words, you don't know that your nickname is "Shots," do you?*

A. *No.*

Q. *You have seen it on this yellow sheet, is that right?*

A. *No.*

Q. *But you never heard that that was your nickname, did you?*

A. *No, as far as I know.*

...

Q. *Well, have you seen this recently? I'm showing you the yellow sheet. Did you see this?...*

A. *Well, I'm just trying to think now.*

Q. *Look at it?*

A. *I think I seen it once.*

Q. *You did see it?*

A. *Yes.*

...

Q. *Do you actually remember the name of the police officer that arrested you,*
   independently, do you remember this?

A. *Yes and no.*

UPON INFORMATION AND BELIEF

In case anyone's bullshit detector is clicking like a gotcha Geiger counter, now's when I'm going to mix my metaphors and hop off the high horse forthwith. Nobody looks good riding up in that type of saddle, and I am no exception. For one thing, and though this may be a low bar, my father never beat the crap out of me, we never ate cat food, and we never slept in a refrigerator-size cardboard box under the expressway overpass. He is not comparable to some insane patriarch drawn from the pages of a weirdly elegant Edward St. Aubyn novel, a sick, sadistic, predatory man. He did spend a little while in jail, but never served years in a state penitentiary—as my little brother eventually would.

For another thing, he is not blameworthy for *my* questionable choices in adulthood. I'm not setting him up for a shakedown. Fact is, and I'm not proud of it, I myself was not always from the start a model father to my own son. That I was for agonizing stretches a semi-absentee father, similar to how my own father was, is not exactly false—though my deficient participation was sometimes the product of decisions my boy's mother made, such as the time she secretly moved out of state and didn't tell me where he was. Again, I'm not defending myself, and I am no innocent. And I'm not trying to assuage my guilt, either; that is one trick I never mastered.

Suzanne and I lived together about two years and did not marry. In a delusional moment I sincerely proposed and was sincerely rejected, and she summarily kicked me out of the house before the boy's first birthday. Given my track record, I'm not sure any rational person could fault her, but of course I did and vehemently. I was twenty-five and possessed of what would come to be called anger issues. It would take years for some semblance of domestic peace to break out, and for me to acknowledge she was on balance a good mom—what the venerable psychologist D. W. Winnicott calls a "good enough mother," which, if you know your Winnicott the way I do not know Winnicott, you realize is the highest imaginable praise. Now that the boy has become by any measure a successful, balanced adult with his own stable and loving family, rapprochement lingers to this day on both sides of our sentried, mostly devoid-of-IEDs, mutually negotiated DMZ. We all make mistakes, and she and I made some world-class doozies, but few mistakes turn out half as well as ours: a wonderful child. Hindsight is both a bitch and a blessing, even if it takes a lifetime to savor.

As a father I answered the bell in time, and before my son turned nine or ten, I was no longer absent and was continually on the job; after I filed suit to establish paternity and claim parental rights, his mother and I set about sharing joint legal custody. My lawyer said that the judge was impressed; he had probably never ruled on the case of a man suing to be the father and therefore to willingly provide child support. It was usually the mother going after a deadbeat whose swimmers had made a successful beachhead. My attorney did add that, since I made the tactical error of wearing a nice suit to court, my child support dollars probably ratcheted up a bit. I was relieved and thankful she never contested my paternity, and I never had the slightest doubt, either. I never had an interest in doing one of those DNA swab tests. I knew he was my boy from the moment he was born while I was wearing my delivery room green scrubs at Kaiser in San Francisco. And to be fair, I should add that she was nothing less than a champ during the strenuous, twenty-nine-hour labor, and I was nothing but the hapless so-called birth coach. My conviction was underscored when my son was probably nine or so, after he met a dicey associate of mine and offered his opinion: "I don't trust him, he's too sincere." That's my boy.

Some people cannot believe the next part; sometimes I have difficulty myself. As it turned out, decades after Brooklyn I did publish a couple of honest-to-God parenting books with a respected

New York publishing house, cowritten with a gifted psychologist friend and colleague, works on child and family development that people actually bought and read and referenced, mostly approvingly. (See under: *irony*.)

∾

LOOKING BACK NOW MANY years, I think anybody would concur the old man nailed it. *Whaddayou, writin' a book?* It wasn't the first time, and it wouldn't be the last, that he nailed it.

I kept my father company very late in his transplanted California life, spending more time with him as he was approaching his final square-up day than I ever did as a child. I remained an irritatingly inquisitive adult. I didn't let up. He wanted to know why I continued to bug him with my questions. I told him the truth, that I was trying to remember.

"Yeah, well, I'm trying to forget."

Who could fault him for trying?

Still: nice try, chief.

∾

IT'S NOT MY TASK, and not my responsibility, to judge my father. It will be demonstrated that I already have a full-time occupation judging myself. Nonetheless, that's an ultimately resistible side-benefit, what comes with the territory of being any man's son, in my case a son who trades in words on the page. As I reflect and examine the clues littering the trails, I can also visualize the crime scene chalk lines of desperation that marked him, and I empathize. More surprising, I can also see, occasionally if not universally to my disappointment, unexpected connections between his life choices—and his afflictions—and my own. Similar to him, I have been broke more than once, I was a professional gambler, I took my share of dumb jobs, I was targeted by law enforcement, I've had my own nasty chemical dependency. Fun times. Not quite.

As for being antisocial, unlike him, I have never been called that, not even by some exes, who could have been justifiably tempted. But I do have an insatiable appetite for separation and solitude. I'm no Zen master, either, and my solitary hours can be crowded as the morning commute train. That's when my brain is bustling with those imaginary companions who populate my fictions and poems, figures who both resemble and are nothing like me, but they all talk my ear off. I also spent many years in that meta-public arena known as schools, taking classes or acquiring academic degrees or teaching, with some small if measurable success, it might be argued. I exhibited a curmudgeonish streak in faculty meetings, but later in life I learned to squelch that, after realizing that was a bad bet. And I was never cynical with or about my students. They more often than not made my day. So maybe not antisocial, more like a monk who gets around town a lot.

～

"IT WAS TRUE AT the time."

Welcome to Downtown Joe Di Prisco, my father, whose street name was, as I mentioned, Pope, or Popey. Unlike the Vicar of Jesus Christ and Supreme Pontiff and Bishop of Rome, his infallibility was never a matter of dogma, except perhaps in his own mind. He was a compulsive gambler and someone who may or may not have been a bookmaker himself, and he was a small-time criminal and, as previously stipulated, in the eyes of observers an "unsavory character." (I'm pretty sure, unlike with *antisocial*, my exes would have voiced that last opinion about me.)

As I would come to discover, he owned up to at least some of his crimes and the crimes of others for reasons that, on their face, sometimes indeed appear to be undeniably ass-covering, expedient, and perhaps ethically suspect.

I think many of us could step up and take a number. I know I could.

More pertinently, at least for me, and, as the billable-hour lawyers reliably qualify, "upon information and belief," I set about the task of decoding the complex and compelling and profoundly mundane pressures bearing down on him—ones that stole us to California in the first place.

NEW YORK STATE APPELLATE DIVISION

RECORDS AND BRIEFS

Q. *Did you remain inside the truck?*

A. *Yes, sir.*

Q. *What happened then?*

A. *Well, we noticed a lot of people running around, and I noticed this one fellow, Bagooch, Mike Gallo.*

Q. *What observation did you make of him?*

A. *Well, he appeared on the scene, and then he got in this car, and he came by the truck, and he looked at the truck, just to see if he could see the driver, and then he went away.*

Q. *Did Santa, did you see Santa do anything?*

A. *Well, he hid his face with his hands.*

Q. *Now, this fellow Bagooch, M-a-g-o-o-c-h, is he any relation to Cock-eyed Jerry?*

A. *He was his partner.*

Q. *Partner in what?*

A. *Bookmaking.*

Q. *Now, what happened?*

A. *Well, I told Patrolman Santa that he better take me away.*

Q. *And did he?*

A. *Yes, sir.*

Q. *And where did he drive you?*

A. *Greenpoint.*

Q. *Where did he drive to?*

A. *Greenpoint Avenue and North Henry Street.*

Q. *Was that the place of the meeting?*

A. *Yes, sir.*

Q. *And what happened there?*

A. *Well, we waited, and about an hour or so later, Patrolman Peter Celentano, Frisher, and Gallagher appeared, and they told us they found the work. Patrolman Celentano said that he found the work, and they scored for a thousand dollars.*

Q. *Did they say where they found the work?*

A. *Yes.*

Q. *Where?*

A. *It was outside the toilet.*

Q. *Did he say how it got there?*

A. *Well, his mother went into the toilet.*

Q. *Whose mother?*

A. *Cock-eyed Jerry's mother, and he didn't hear the water flush, so she come out, and he went in, and he was looking for the slips.*

Q. *Did he tell you anything else?*

A. *Well, they scored him for a thousand dollars.*

Q. *What did he say?*

A. *He said, "We agreed to let him go for a thousand dollars."*

INCRIMINATIONS

At the risk of sounding glib—and this is one risk I have no alternative but to take—my father's experience does not seem totally unconnected to the small-time author of a memoir, his son, who shares his first and last name along with some related compulsions (if not his ecclesiastic street name). A memoir capitalizes on the repositories of memory, the moveable treasure chests locatable throughout multiple corners and nooks and crannies inside the circuitry of the brain, and it deals in disclosure, in risking confidences and self-exposure, in telling the truth about oneself and others as far as it can be known. The unexamined life may well be, as some wise guy once said, not worth living. But what about the overexamined life? If you're not reckless enough, it might not be worth writing about.

As for mundane pressure, a memoir writer registers that in spades. Publish a memoir, lose a friend or two, infuriate somebody, bank on it. And endure questions from strangers at book talks such as: "Who are you to write a memoir?" and "Why should anybody care?"

In such moments, I always wish I could quote my serpent-tongued mother when she advised me during her pugilistic social life: *You remember, sonny boy, rude is not funny.* Then again, she never would have uttered much less subscribed to such an axiom.

Memoir writers confess and they confide as they may or must, and what a world of difference between the two. As Emily Fox Gordon lucidly explains, the entity or person to whom (or which) one confesses has "the power to condemn, punish, absolve, or forgive." Whereas "[c]onfidences are offered to equals, or at least the offering and accepting of confidences places the two parties involved on equal terms." In any case, confessing and/or confiding as they do, nobodies have lives, too, and if they're lucky, or unlucky, enough, have a tale to tell, which their memoirs will have the burden to prove one way or another.

In *Subway to California*, published in 2014, I ranged around my childhood recollections in Brooklyn and its challenges through my adulthood missteps in California, my education and my teaching career, my experience as a professional card player, my time in a Catholic religious order, my failures in love and academia, my coming to terms (or largely not) with loss, my anxiety, my life as a writer and husband and father. It also prominently treats my unfinished relationships with family members, and the mysteries that persisted unresolved after, one by one, they died.

When you publish a memoir as I did, unanticipated consequences routinely occur. As many authors of memoirs attest, the genre encourages personal boundary encroachment. Reviewers are one species, people you know, or don't know, another. Those people will say anything. Often, if not always, to your face. Maybe that's understandable, and that's life in the big city.

About some interested parties you do unambivalently care for and about, you wonder if you struck the grace notes you intended. I should qualify. You wonder, that is, if you're somebody self-mortifying like me. And *wonder*'s not the word, more like *obsess*. Then, of course, there was the distant relation who posted nasty stuff about me and my book on Facebook, so I obviously hit the pitch perfect note there, and he was satisfyingly bug-be-gone zapped into cyberspace, and that's more than enough airtime for the sourpuss. Some of my droller friends demanded to know how come they weren't in the damn book they paid good money for, but as another friend and graduate school colleague wrote, "This is finally the guy we knew we never knew." I don't know how to defend my choices (for starters it wasn't an autobiography), or what to tell them, except this: take a look at the dedication page of this book in your hands. All in all, reactions on the personal front ran the gamut. For instance, my Catholic boys' high school blood rival told a mutual friend I never respected him because he wasn't Italian. (Here I thought my best friends in school were named Fredotovich, Gray, Hooper, Marmolejo, and Reed.) And then this: a most significant ex, with whom I shared a long-term, volatile if life-defining relationship that unraveled insanely and cinematically, rocked me. "We remember such different things," she wrote me in an out-of-the-blue email. Fair enough, if chilling. She didn't come off as tarnished as I did in that book of mine, but nevertheless: that was stunningly gracious on the part of somebody who, though her identity was concealed, might have wanted a piece of me. (If by the off-chance you are reading this, and you know who you are, please don't sue me.) Her kind appraisal of the book shook me and continues to resonate. And I also heard from many former students, and theirs were often the most moving, gratifying messages. But there was my college girlfriend, too, first-love and all, who didn't talk to me for a couple of years. I can explain, and as you will see, she will play a major role in this story.

ONCE THOSE COURT TRANSCRIPTS materialized, I was nourished with manna from Google. As we know, it was manna that unexpectedly fell from the sky to sustain those wanderers in the desert looking for the Promised Land. As for me, I didn't know from promised lands, which as far as I understood did not exist along the bus lines in

Williamsburg, and I would have needed a guide dog to wend my way to la de dah Park Slope or the Upper East Side.

Equipped with those transcripts, I did set out to uncover the central mystery that had dogged me my whole life. Gradually, I inched closer and closer to unveiling the heretofore concealed predicate for our exile out of Brooklyn as well as the untold story of my father's life—and its connections to my younger brother's as well.

As is often the case, the unknown has a way of leading to other unknowns, secrets to more secrets.

Following the map of my father's steps from the past, I am by turns alarmed, horrified, astonished, intrigued, baffled. Sometimes I am entertained, and sometimes impressed. From Brooklyn hustler to somebody who held respectable blue-collar jobs for thirty years in California: that bare bones summary does not tell the whole story. And some jaundiced types might suggest that his last full-time position, elected leader of a Teamster union local, was borderline respectable at best. The FBI itself was skeptical and they launched an investigation into his activities. More later.

∽

F. SCOTT FITZGERALD WRITES in the opening to *The Great Gatsby* that Gatsby "…turned out all right in the end; it is what preyed on Gatsby, what foul dust floated in the wake of his dreams…"—that's the intuition that moved Nick Carraway to tell his story, or so he claims.

Carraway begins by remarking that he has been turning over in his mind his father's advice: to never forget that other people haven't had his advantages. In my instance, I myself have been turning over in my mind things my father said but, somehow more, things he never said.

My old man didn't own a mansion on West Egg, Long Island, didn't cultivate Gatsby's grand romantic designs or wear "such beautiful shirts" (he religiously stuck with his racetrack standard-issue polos). Carraway of New Haven and I probably don't have much in common either, though we both seem fascinated by the shadow lives of criminals, but no, as far as I know, my dad did not attempt to fix a horse race or the World Series. True, he was chased by cops into the woods of East Islip, Long Island, but he never gravitated to the Hamptons, never put on so much as a little cocktail party, and his dreams were sometimes as impenetrable for me.

Did the borderline-okay Di Prisco turn out all right in the end? Again, the answer is yes and no, and besides, *Who wantsta know?* Maybe in the end Pope and I both "beat on, boats against the current, borne back ceaselessly into the past"—much like every writer of a memoir. And maybe like everybody else.

It could be that I am overthinking this. I've been accused of that, and much worse, before. Perhaps it's simpler in my case. Everybody knows what Joan Didion notoriously and perceptively wrote: "Writers are always selling somebody out." Maybe selling out oneself and others runs in a family fathered by an informant.

Whaddayou, writin' a book?

When my father testified, he occasionally invoked his Fifth Amendment rights, so as not to incriminate himself. I don't believe such rights are available to the writer of a memoir.

New York State Appellate Division

RECORDS AND BRIEFS

Q. *What did the work entail?*

A. *Turning up bookmakers.*

Q. *And when you say, "Turning up bookmakers," what do you mean?*

A. *Well, I would tell—I would more or less tell a police officer about where a bookmaker was working, or where he would keep the slips, and things like that.*

Infinitely Dropped

Once, in the 1990s, we were traveling in the drifting snow, coming up the mountains, heading for Lake Tahoe. I had a new, brawny Jeep, but my dad complained I was driving too fast. "Slow down," he said, being an inveterate backseat driver including while riding shotgun. I reminded him I had four-wheel drive and was not close to an unsafe speed. He was unimpressed: "Yeah, but this ain't no magic carpet."

That trip was remarkable, to me, for another thing he said. When I was driving up to the hotel I did something—cannot recall what it was—he said I shouldn't do. Then he reconsidered and realized what I did was all right. "Sorry," he said. What's noteworthy is that that is the one and only time I can recall he ever said to me he was sorry about anything. I did not feel vindicated or satisfied. It wasn't some moment I'd been waiting for all my life. No, in the instant, I was a little bit astounded and—honestly—worried for him, as his apology was so out of character. If I were still in therapy, that incident might have made for a productive session. As for my mother's apologies, she never caught up with my father in the "I'm sorry" department, because she never admitted being wrong in her life. Perhaps she couldn't risk an apology, thereby revealing what must have felt, to her, like weakness.

⌒

As I REFLECT ON my sociopathic and depressed and self-absorbed parents, now both buried in New York, it becomes clearer that truth and truthfulness were existentially contestable, or dismissible, propositions for them. All the same, they were larger-than-life, charismatic figures—at least so they seemed to me as a boy. Despite scuffling throughout their lives, they were so glamorous they might have been the once-upon-a-time Brad and Angelina of my Greenpoint neighborhood. But given *their* break-up, that's already an anachronistic cultural signifier. Think instead Bogie and Bacall. *You know how to whistle, don't you? You put your lips together and blow.*

My Polish mother was variously called Catherine, or Kay, or Caza (pronounced Ka-sza, short for her given name, Cashmera). Her sepia-tone photos show that she was quite the stunner and, by reputation in her own family, she was a party-girl flirt. She was also a liar of genius, a manipulator par excellence. She never backed down from a street fight, being someone who viscerally communicated that she may not come out victorious in a skirmish, but she would not circumvent conflict, and if she were to be vanquished, the winner would bear scorch marks for souvenirs.

My father's catch-all counsel for living, passed down to me from the earliest days: *Don't take no shit from nobody.* Into his eighties he would defend his wife's combativeness by saying she was temperamentally a junkyard dog, and he was heartbreakingly good-looking in his own right and had his own longstanding challenges with fact. My mom said that he would lie even when the truth was on his side. Based upon my own experience, I can verify that was at least one time *she* was not lying. They were in many respects a perfect match, and theirs was a marriage made, if not in heaven, in the legendary Brooklyn of the *dese* and *dose, fuggetaboutit, shut the fuck up* fifties and sixties.

D. W. Winnicott once wrote an essay on "The Effect of Psychotic Parents." I'm no shrink, but I've paid many a shrink's bills, and I wouldn't suggest that my parents qualified as exactly psychotic. He makes some sense to me, especially about my mother:

"Depression may be a chronic illness, giving a parent a poverty of available affect, or it may be a serious illness appearing in phases, with more or less sudden withdrawal of rapport… An infant in this position feels infinitely dropped."

Infinitely dropped: there's an image I will roll around in my mind. He goes on to theorize more pointedly:

"Children can deal, therefore, with mood swings in their parents by carefully observing them, but it is the unpredictability of some parents that can be traumatic. Once children have come through the earliest stages of maximal dependence, it seems to me that they can come to terms with almost any adverse factor that remains constant or that can be predicted."

And I could do that, too. However adverse the home factors might have been, they did become almost predictable. Nothing seemed more unforeseeable, and paradoxically downright normal, than my father skipping town that summer. Beyond that, to be precise, daily life proceeded like clockwork: my father comes back from the track, busted, my mother goes nuts. My father's depressed, my mother's furious. My father disappears, my mother plots revenge. Winnicott continues:

"Naturally, children with high intelligence have an advantage over those with low intelligence in this matter of prediction, but sometimes we find that the intellectual powers of highly intelligent children have been overstrained—the intelligence has been prostituted in the cause of predicting complex parental moods and tendencies."

I don't know how high my intelligence is now or was at five or ten, but it was definitely overstrained, so hold that thought. Who knows, being overstrained might be a functional definition of a writer.

My good friend is a real-life rocket scientist. "Everybody thinks that rocket science is hard," he once said to me. "You know what's hard? Being a parent." He didn't need to mention the obvious corollary: same is true for a child.

Hold that thought, too.

∽

THE CLOUDS IMMEDIATELY PARTED when I found in 2015, post-parental-mortem, those court records. I finally was in possession of some undeniable facts. Facts can be good. For one thing, they are facts. Even in this postmodern age, when facts and opinions blur and blend into each other on talking-head television shows or in political debates as well as in Departments of Philosophy, matters on the public record are, you know, on the public record. If I learned how to use the newly acquired information, I might be on my way beyond my parents' deceptions and nondisclosures and secrets, and beyond the facts to the holy grail of the truth I missed as a child.

But *Holy Grail*? That might be exaggerating the goal. Growing up, I was unacquainted with fables or knight errant legends, but even ten-year-old Brooklyn kids have somehow already seen it all, or blithely convinced themselves as much. Therefore I might have intuited that quests for such a thing as a holy grail end up with nothing more than a junky, cracked mug. Funny how these new facts constituted the beginning of another, just as important, search into my own life.

It's often been said that the great gift for a child who becomes a writer is a miserable childhood. I can see the point, though I never felt adequately grateful to thank my parents. One thing I did come away with as a child was that my parents wouldn't tell me the truth or that they didn't know or that they didn't care or that it didn't matter, and I'm not sure to this day which is preferable, or if these distinctions are worthy to be distinguished. I have made a very modest career of creating fictions of my own, in novels and poems as well as in my life. I used to spend many a fifty-minute hour in one talk therapist's office after another narrating my story of my story. In actuality, long ago as an adult, I had my own run-ins with law enforcement and cultivated an addiction of my own, and so did my brother John, which in his case eventuated in a tragic conclusion. Now late in my own life, the jury remains out. I have been conducting a hunt for clues to my clueless family and to the origins of my clueless self, because where else do we first shape notions about ourselves if not in our families?

In childhood my Brooklyn world was not a song lifting up in the sunlit room, fields not rippling gold, skies not reliably big and electric blue. But that's okay, because *that* was the gift, such as it was, in the end. I didn't grow up in Downton Abbey, but let's be clear, it wasn't *Game of Thrones*, either. But *Goodfellas*, or *Donnie Brasco*, which was a movie shot not very far away in the old neighborhood? Maybe a little bit, with *The Honeymooners* thrown in.

From the first, I became intimately acquainted with shadows and darkness and rage and absence and chaos, awareness of which I perhaps somewhat perversely cherished. That awareness proved indispensable. I didn't find peace and light and music and presence at home. I did find it elsewhere: in school and in my pious little boy's religious faith. That's where I plumbed the psalms and stories and rituals and parables in order to locate the coherence and integrity that I otherwise lacked—and yearned for. A destabilized childhood provides somebody who grows up to be a writer, like me, the opportunity, and the urgent invitation, to lay an imaginative foundation for one's own life. If I didn't do that, who would?

∽

WATCH OUT NOW, STEP lively. Here's where Jesus crashes the party on the waterfront. That rabble-rousing, metaphorical-sword-swinging shit-kicker rides in—without my consciously registering as much—to rescue my small Catholic self. To quote chapter and verse:

"Whoever comes to me and does not hate father and mother, wife and children, brothers and sisters, yes, and even life itself, cannot be my disciple." (Luke 14: 26)

"Someone told him, 'Look, your mother and your brothers are standing outside, waiting to speak to you.' But to the one who told him this, Jesus replied. 'Who is my mother, and who are my brothers?' And pointing to his disciples, he said, 'Here are my mother and my brothers! For whoever does the will of my Father in heaven is my brother and sister and mother.'" (Matthew 12: 47-50)

"Do not think that I have come to bring peace to the earth; I have come not to bring peace, but a sword. For I have come to set a man against his father, and a daughter against her mother, and a daughter-in-law against her mother-in-law, and one's foes will be members of one's household. Whoever loves father or mother more than me is not worthy of me, and whoever loves son or daughter more than me is not worthy of me, and whoever does not take up the cross and follow me is not worthy of me. Those who find their life will lose it, and whoever who lose their life for my sake will find it." (Matthew 10: 34-39)

Harsh, bracing stuff, if construed literally. Maybe He with a capital H was speaking elliptically—and when was He *not* speaking in parable and why would He bother to do otherwise? From early on, I grasped that Jesus was never fucking around. Theologians and saints universally agree on that point, though they usually phrase it somewhat differently. It's all or nothing. When He says hate and lose the family, the Religion class teachers would doubtless qualify that Jesus is exaggerating for effect, yanking his audience's chain, nothing more, because elsewhere He makes clear we should honor mother and father. Not sure I am buying that, quite. I have no recollection of ever reflecting on those scriptural verses as a child, or ever hearing them, but I'm not swayed that matters much. I swallowed whole the olive, pit and all. Jesus' message was, yes, you need your family, but you need Me more. Maybe I could work with that, for a while.

⬿

PAGING DR. WINNICOTT.

"Artists are people driven by the tension between the desire to communicate and the desire to hide."

"Tell me what you fear and I will tell you what has happened to you."

"For the five children in a family there are five families. It does not require a psychoanalyst to see that these five families need not resemble each other, and are certainly not identical."

Dr. Winnicott?

⬿

AS FOR TRUTH-TELLING, AND more importantly, truth-knowing, if not now, when?

My father might have enjoyed the mixed blessings of having the last word in his son's book—though I doubt it, and besides, if he did enjoy something he would never explicitly own up to it. It might be the case that the most memoir writers can affirm, in good faith, about the story of their lives they are telling is that, for what it's worth, when they get it right, it was true at the time.

New York State Appellate Division

RECORDS AND BRIEFS

Q. You might have said fifty?

A. I possibly said fifty.

Q. Why would you say fifty if it was a hundred?

A. I just came back from California.

Q. Anything in California to refresh the memory?

A. I left the family behind.

Q. Now, how does it refresh the memory?

A. At the time it did.

Joseph DiPrisco, for Department, Direct

Q. Now, what exactly happened in March, late March, of 1961, with this bookmaker you mentioned? A. Well, I had a bookmaker by the name of cock-eyed Jerry.

Q. Cock-eyed Jerry? A. Yes, and he worked on the corner of North 7 Driggs Avenue.

Q. In Brooklyn? A. In Brooklyn, yes. And I gave this information to Jim Santa, and he made an appointment to meet—later meet Patrolman Peter Celentano.

Q. Where did you meet?

Dep. Com. Reisman: Did you meet?

A. Yes, sir, for me to meet Patrolman Peter Celentano.

Q. And where did you meet? A. Greenpoint Avenue.

Q. Now, did you mention—

Dep. Com. Reisman: With whom did you meet him?

A. I met with Patrolman Peter Celentano, Jim Santa, Patrolman Gallagher, and Dave Frischer.

Q. Now, when you gave this information out about cock-eyed Jerry, did you also give him any information as to the means of transportation? A. Yes, sir.

Q. What was that? A. They had to get a truck, I spoke to Jim Santa.

Q. Why was that? A. Well, you couldn't get on the block without being noticed, he had to be in a truck.

Q. Now, when you met the person you just mentioned, and where did you meet them? A. Greenpoint Avenue and North Henry Street, in Brooklyn.

Q. In Brooklyn? What did you observe when you met? A. Well, they had a truck with them, and Peter Celentano, and Gallagher, and Frischer, and Santa, were there.

Q. And did you convey information about this Jerry? A. Yes, sir.

1961

My father died on the evening of July 3, 2012. Thirty months later I discovered he had been extradited more than fifty years earlier from California to New York on September 28, 1961. As a child, I wouldn't have appreciated the legal implications had I been armed with such information, and I wasn't. Accounts vary as to whether he himself contacted authorities in New York to give himself up after being indicted in Brooklyn and Queens, or if he had been tracked down. This would be the first of his several trips to New York to testify. There appeared in the long-ago-defunct *Berkeley Gazette* a couple-of-square-inch news article with a tiny boldface headline on the order of FBI ARRESTS BERKELEY MAN, which my father carried around in his wallet for I believe a long time. One day he pulled it out and showed me; I cannot recall exactly when or under what circumstances. I didn't understand its import, and if I asked him to elucidate, he did not say anything I can remember.

All I recall for certain of that September 28 day—and I recall this vividly—were the two stolid men in trench coats and fedoras who showed up on our apartment landing in California one morning and escorted him away. Away where? I had no idea as to his destination or his return. I asked my mother, who was chain-smoking disconsolately at the kitchen table and sipping a cup of coffee with lots of cream and sugar, which is how she preferred. She couldn't or wouldn't illuminate me. Her two strongest moves to the bucket: screaming and silence.

Once or twice, late in his life, he vaguely intimated to me that he was fearful a hit had been put out on him. As I would come to learn, he had implied the same earlier to my older half-brothers. This supposed threat might have been conceivably the product of his penchant for theatrics or his paranoia, but I am not so sure—especially when I factor in that he lived in Serpico times, when there were more than a few unscrupulous and dangerous and eminently indictable cops on the beat. I might discount the very notion if he ever belabored or sensationalized this anxiety, but he never did. He was usually not candid, to put it mildly, but he was always more trustworthy when being vague and reluctant to talk, when self-revelations needed to be pried from him. His very imprecision was a marker of the closest he got to honesty. I know he adamantly avoided New York for many, many years after the trials, to the extent of not attending his own parents' funerals, which took place not long after his testifying. When he traveled to the city to be a witness they sequestered him in a hotel, kept him under guard of the Police Commissioner's Confidential Investigations Unit. "They took care of me," he said. In such an atmosphere, it doesn't seem far-fetched to speculate that the badge-wearing, gun-toting cops he sold out, or their associates, would seek an opening for reprisals, not to mention the bookmakers and other criminals whose names he had named. He never assumed another identity, so wasn't he a sitting duck in California? Come to think of it, weren't we also? It's a big country, but not Siberia. On the other hand, under continual cross-examination as to his current whereabouts, he took the Fifth, and the PCCIU stood behind him, refusing to disclose where he lived.

ᔛ

HISTORICAL-CULTURAL COLOR MIGHT PROVIDE some useful context for his activities. So what was happening around that time on the great stage of the world? (Not that I am implying I was fully aware of what was going on then.)

Well, first of all, on the great stage of *my* world I am a sixth-grader at Saint Stanislaus Kostka School, in Greenpoint, till June 1961. In September, I matriculate, a seventh-grader, at Saint Joseph the Workman School (as it was then called), in Berkeley. Spiffy school uniform: green cardigan, white short-sleeve shirt, salt-and-pepper corduroys. Eat your heart out, Barney's. In California, Sister

Euphemia, a witty and lovely human being, is a gifted, kind teacher. I'm the youngest in the class, owing to the fact that I had skipped the second grade. There are African American kids in my class, a new social and academic experience as I had never met a black kid in my life, and some become friends. I pick up a basketball for the first time. I also strike out in a kickball game, a dubious feat so far almost certainly unreplicated in recorded preadolescent human history.

JFK inaugurated. Catholics kicking ass, taking numbers. Robert Frost (whose words these are I think I know) recites a poem (supposedly) in the freezing cold. We watch the ceremony on TV in class. The new president, defiantly not wearing a hat, delivers his unforgettably eloquent (and possibly the most bellicose in history) inaugural address.

Pope John XXIII starts blowing the house up and the Catholic Church promises never to be the same. I don't believe John XXIII's street name is "Pope," which is already taken.

(I am aware of the existence of at least one other street-named "Pope," which was the nickname of Michele Greco, the frighteningly notorious *mafioso*. He makes his appearance in Alexander Stille's *Excellent Cadavers*, a stunning, stomach-churning study of Sicilian magistrates and the Cosa Nostra. Read it and weep, and I mean that. You will never again be tempted to lionize the mafia. Excellent cadavers? *Cadaveri eccellenti* was how they characterized the trophy assassinations of public figures like politicians and magistrates, and not to be confused with the routine killings of run-of-the-mill mobsters.)

Bay of Pigs.

Nuremburg Trials. Adolph Monster Eichman. Hannah Arendt coins "the banality of evil." She's in bed, in both senses, with Nazi sympathizer Martin Heidegger, whose iconic works become my intellectual touchstone in college and beyond.

Freedom Riders in the Deep South. Sit-ins in the Shallow North. Martin Luther King emerging. Malcolm X. Civil Rights.

Cold War.

Berlin Wall.

Nikita Kruschev pounds his shoe at the United Nations and is going to bury us. He hates tying laces, so it was a loafer; no details as to the color of his Red Communist socks. We regularly dive under school desks, practicing for the inevitable Russian atomic bomb.

Bomb shelters proliferate.

(This brings up a much later association. In high school, I have a pal who, when he gets in trouble, which is habitually, is banished to the basement where his punishment is to dig in the family bomb shelter. We keep him around not entirely, completely, totally because his sister is excruciatingly foxy. He also has beer access and keys to a functioning car. At some point I get a part-time job in a busy department store selling women's shoes. Don't go there, it was real money for an on-commission teenager, at least till the women returned them the following week, as they maddeningly would, and my next paycheck was docked. All of us sales*men* every day spill out of a clown car and punch in. There is one sales*woman*, but insofar as her cutthroat marketing style makes me think of bloodthirsty, spurned women in Greek tragedies, she fits in. Otherwise, they are mumblers and chain-smokers, yucksters and conmen, partial to wearing cheap suits and skinny clip-on ties, their dragon breath a noxious bittersweet blend of Dentyne and coffee. The undisputed stars and big earners of the sales staff are two suspiciously overqualified, extremely intelligent and mordant middle-age unctuous fellows who compete with and detest each other. One lights up every opportunity in the stock room and leaves a smoldering cigarette to char the edges of every available shelf when he hustles back onto the floor to complete the sale and get a leg up on his nemesis. He is a supremely confident explainer, by which I mean he answers customers' questions and concerns about the wares in a professional-sounding esoteric way no one could either contest or comprehend, but it does the trick: customers line up at the *cha ching*ing cash register. The other gent, who is somehow more oleaginous, wears the same suit every shift, but is magically never less than supremely presentable. He speaks in complete paragraphs with an indefinable and perhaps fake Southern accent, which charms the gals, and vents his Satanic sneering contempt for them once he slips and slides off the floor into the back room. He has one joke he has seemingly perfected in the course of his life. A customer who would like his attention inquires, "Are you free?" and he replies, "No, but I'm cheap." I didn't hazard the following diagnostic supposition at the time, but here goes. Sure, everybody needed a job, but my purely indefensible speculation now is those two smart slicksters might have been foot-fetishists. Not that that is wrong, I am supposed to say. But if so, what a field day they enjoyed, because the money couldn't have been adequate to satisfy some deep yearning, which was more ungraspable to me than the tender soles of women sacrificing themselves on the altar of their monetized desire. Anyway, in the Women's and Ladies' Shoe Department, as I called it, my personal professional shoe sales high point takes place when my friend's foxy sister dances in one Saturday afternoon. Her foot measured a perfect slender seven, I *think*, and she was wearing a white mini, I *know*. See? No *foot* fetish for me—yet. This moment replays thereafter in the all-night theater of my favorite, eventful dreams. I hoped she would soon bring back her shoes so we could do this *pas de deux* do-oeuvre all over again, hell with the commission. One other minor mystery lingers—not that I was ever hired in the first place, no, that's more like nobody else suitably psychologically wounded wanted the job. More than a couple of times I waited on ladies or women who insisted they were, say, a six, or whatever, and when they tried on the

six, or whatever, it was obvious to my male or masculine eyes they
were in reality eights or nines because, look, their feet sloshed out,
sides and toes and heels beyond the islands of their soles. But they
purchased the smaller, constraining, more beautiful shoes anyway.
This was a valuable lesson I learned that I still don't understand. Wait.
Was that why my return rate was so high?) Now back to our regularly
scheduled program.

Cars with fins, resembling spaceships probably hovering over the
moonlit East River.

*West Side Story, Breakfast at Tiffany's, The Hustler, La Dolce Vita,
The Parent Trap.*

Ribbon cutting on the new BQE. (The Brooklyn-Queens
Expressway, of course, for the instructional benefit of you rush-hour
Californians stuck on the Golden Gate Bridge or the Four Oh Five
into El A.)

Peace Corps created.

Russian astronaut, first human in space.

South Africa: apartheid, the law of the accursed land.

First US military involvement (as "advisers") in Vietnam.

First disposable diaper, Pampers.

Gallon of gas: twenty-seven cents.

VW Beetle. Chevy Impala. Ford Thunderbird.

Patsy Cline: "I Fall to Pieces." Forty-five rpm records rule.

Catch-22, To Kill a Mockingbird, Franny & Zooey, Tropic of Cancer.

Among the Dangs, National Book Award short list; beautiful short stories by George P. Elliott, my future college professor, earliest writing advocate, friend and mentor. To this day, miss him like water.

Wagon Train, Gunsmoke, Perry Mason, The Andy Griffith Show.

Brooklyn Fucking Dodgers now the Los Angeles Fucking Dodgers: forevermore dead to me.

As in Greenpoint, I become an altar boy in Berkeley, and remain a pious tyke, albeit one who shoplifts and secretly studies smutty word-picture books that masterbatefully use words like "stiff shaft" and "perky boobs" and "areola" (had to look up that one in my trusty big swinging dictionary), paperback tomes lifted from the corner drugstore mass market rack. (Rack, another useful word, different context.) The shop owner notifies the school—guess the boychik thief's green uniform was the first clue as to the reprobate's identity. Sister Euphemia puts the whole class on salvation alert, chillingly advising us: don't do anything you wouldn't do in front of the Blessed Virgin Mary. (Cheap shot, but potent enough.) Big picture: the Church is about to undergo a sweet bloodless revolution called Vatican II, though the Jews are universally guilty of killing Our Lord and Savior Jesus Christ. But then the Jews are deemed not guilty anymore of killing Jesus. My first real girlfriend in college is Jewish and Manhattan-born and –bred and almost every single one of the legion of talk therapists I eventually bore to tears as an adult are Jewish; no idea what all that means for my guilt-ridden, smut-stained soul.

I make my first basketball shot, on an asphalt court in Berkeley. I would go on to spend the rest of my extensive, undistinguished basketball career on one outdoor court or gym or another, never passing up a shot whether I was open or not. As a former student once asked me after he heard I blew out my ACL in a game: how the hell did you hurt yourself when all you do is stand outside the three-point line begging for the ball?

Melvin picks a fight with me on the court. By rep he reigns as biggest badass of the tough-as-tuna-fish-salad elementary school. I had mixed it up on Greenpoint streets, but I had never tussled with a black kid before. Judges split on the result, though I argue I am victorious on points; egos and faces are bruised but we're not on the waterfront and nobody bellows "I coulda been a contenduh," and no blood is spilled before a teacher pulls us apart and tells us to go to our corners. He and I would become friends. Kids, right?

∽

NINETEEN SIXTY-ONE, THEN, WAS the year the Di Priscos had packed in a hurry, left no forwarding address, and neglected to throw themselves a bon voyage party. They traveled under the radar as long as they could. In strictly demographic terms, such a departure was hardly strange. True, during the 1960s the population of New York, the

Empire State, increased by 8 percent, from 16,782,304 to 18,190,740. In that same period, the population of Brooklyn dipped, from 2,627,319 to 2,601,612. Census-takers didn't need an oracle to predict a drop was coming. Once upon a time, 1950, there were 2,738,175 Brooklynites sucking in diesel and smokestack fumes along with their Lucky Strikes while dodging the trolleys that were fast going the way of the dinosaur. Those were the days. Meanwhile, California was booming. In 1960, the population had been 15,506,974. Ten years later, it was 19,953,134, a 27 percent increase, as the Golden State overtook the Empire State as the most populous in America. In fact, between 1950 and 1970 the populace of California had nearly doubled, assisted by the contribution of more than a few New Yorkers who gravitated toward the promise of money, mild winters, endless summers, and perpetual suntan that awaited them on the West Coast. They included Duke Snider and the Brooklyn Dodgers, who became the *Los Angeles* Dodgers in 1958. That was the same year their blood rivals, Willie Mays and the New York Giants, became the *San Francisco* Giants. Vengefully, I adopt the Giants as *my* team. During the sixties, while Brooklyn was shedding inhabitants, it so happened that the population of Berkeley, California, was growing almost 5 percent, from 111,268 to 116,716. At least four of the former citizens of Brooklyn defected to Berkeley in the Fall of 1961. As arrivals go, theirs was as uneventful as could be. No ticker tape parade up University Avenue took place, no ribbon-cutting, no keys to the municipality. Joseph Di Prisco, age thirty-five, and Catherine Di Prisco, age thirty-seven, were husband and wife on their way elsewhere, with two young boys in tow. Joe and Kay were not the typical Commie pinko, jazz-hound, beret-topped, reefer-mad agitators and activists that Berkeley had been famous for. They were political inactivists of the first order. For instance, they had never voted. They had never thought of voting, not because they were anarchists, but because they apparently never thought of voting. And they were not academics or artists, and neither had much in the way of school experience. In this regard, and in numerous others, the college town of Berkeley was as wildly improbable a destination for this family as any on the planet. Borneo, Brazil, Bermuda, Beirut, Burma, or the Bastille and Babylonia would have made as much if not more sense. In some other respects, theirs was the ordinary, familiar story of transplantation to California, the land of opportunity. This small family was starting over on the opposite coast. Ordinary as the story may have been, there was nothing simple about what they did or why they did it. As students learn in history class, the United States of America is the setting, and sometimes the devastating cause, and sometimes the grand inspiration of great migrations. *The Grapes of Wrath* comes to mind. As do the hearty tales that echo in the memory vault of Ellis Island, like that of my grandparents. The Di Priscos' story ought not to be confused with any of those. In their more reflective moments, if they occurred, did they let themselves believe they were leaving behind Brooklyn and the past for good? Doubtful, but with them, who can say? Did they allow themselves a glimmer of hope that life was going to be different, perhaps improved? If they knew anything, they had to know better than that. Hope was in short supply around them in Brooklyn, ever since that famous tree growing there caused all those problems and sold all those books. Had hope, had faith, had trust, had worshipful love stopped Duke Snider and the Dodgers from blowing off the most loyal town in America? Of course not. On this score, the Di Priscos were congenitally, perhaps you might say professionally, jaded. Or they were simply deep-down disappointable. Miserable might have been a marker in the family DNA. Anthropologists and ecologists and documentary filmmakers narrate how the geese and the wildebeests and the Monarch butterflies and the sperm whales and so many other species organize themselves to migrate their way across incredible distances—year after year after year. It is a pure wonder. To the expert student of migrating zebras and red crabs, the Di Priscos would have appeared aimless, driven, and a little bit doomed, like glazed-eyed gamblers staring in the face of slot machines all night long in a roadside Nevada casino, waiting for the jackpot bells and whistles that never go off. Yes, they sailed from Brooklyn and yes, they dropped anchor in California. But as sure as the one-arm bandits were going to siphon off the silver dollars in their coin cup, they had no idea what the next move would be. Or the move after that. Or the one after that. Or the one after that. *That* one, that one especially. No, comma, fucking, comma, idea, period.

∽

IN OCTOBER 1961, MY father made his first of several appearances to testify in New York City.

Later, he returns to California. I have no explicit recollection of the homecoming. He spins no tales as we gather around the old fireplace. No fireplace, either.

NEW YORK STATE APPELLATE DIVISION

RECORDS AND BRIEFS

Q. You're under oath?

A. Yes.

Q. You know what that means?

A. I'm not lying.

Q. You're not a liar?

A. I'm not lying.

My Urban Plan

A t one stop along my *Subway to California* book tour, I gave a reading at Diesel Bookstore in fashionable, upscale Brentwood, California. That evening President Obama had descended to hobnob with his bankable big money Hollywood donors up the road, and traffic in the vicinity of the Country Mart was nightmarish, even by LA standards. By the time I started around seven thirty some intrepid souls and local friends along with my publisher and some former students and colleagues and my cherished college-age goddaughter had managed to fight their way inside. People at the bookstore couldn't have been more welcoming, and if the turnout wasn't SRO, the mood was upbeat. I can never forget that I once gave a reading in Virginia during an earlier book tour where exactly one person showed, so I never complain, and I give thanks there are bookstores out there promoting the work of way-less-than-illustrious authors like me. In fact, that night the Diesel Bookstore rep offered a quite beautiful, literate, subtle introduction, which praised the book, but—more importantly—demonstrated she had actually read it. I have travelled on a few book tours and once ran a reading series in a Berkeley bookstore, so I know firsthand that this is a much rarer occurrence for authors and their introducers than is commonly assumed.

At the conclusion of that Brentwood reading, which went all right, I suppose, a business casual woman approached and said fairly pleasantly, or at least without detectible edge, "I am an urban planner. I thought *Subway to California* was a book about public transportation."

Public transportation remains a hot topic in a once-upon-a-time car-mad state the likes of Elon Musk will one day colonize before he does the same on Mars. It's not quite up there with water rights these droughty days, but *really?* I pretended to understand what she said, honest I did—because again, this conversation took place *after* my reading, during which she had not spun on the heels of her Jimmy Choos and stormed out. A little part of me defensibly worried about the future of urban planning in The Golden State.

"So the subway is a metaphor," she continued, "about traveling underground, through darkness?"

"You have no idea," I said.

New York State Appellate Division

RECORDS AND BRIEFS

Q. And what was your conversation with [Officer] Celentano?

A. I asked him about the hundred dollars, if he had it, and I told him I had another bookmaker.

Q. What did he say about the hundred dollars when you asked him?

A. He told me when he got it I would get mine.

Q. Did he say anything else?

A. Yes. And then he told me we start from scratch, being that I told him I had no hard feelings, that I took his money that I owed him.

Q. That he took the money you owed him?

A. Yes, sir. And he said, "We start from scratch."

Q. Was anything else said?

A. Yes, I said I had another bookmaker, and that this fellow was—

Q. Did you mention the bookmaker?

A. Yeah, Junior Loterzio (phonetic).

Q. Did you mention where he operated?

A. He worked for a bank, a policy bank, and he would have these tapes in the car every Sunday, because he would meet runners and give it to them.

Q. What area did he operate in?

A. North Seventh.

Q. Did you tell this to Celentano?

A. Yes, sir.

Q. What did Celentano say?

A. He said, "Let things cool off, you take three thousand dollars out of one neighborhood, that is a lot of money."

Q. And then what happened?

A. Well, then I left.

Q. You left? Now, did there come a time when you met with him again?

A. Yes, sir.

Q. And what date was that?

A. That was April the 15th, it was on a Saturday.

Q. April 15, 1961?

A. Yes, sir.

Q. And how did you get—

A. (Interrupting) I called his office. I wanted to talk to Peter Celentano, and he was in the field, so they asked me to leave a number, and I left a number, and about a half hour later he called me and he said, "Don't say nothing on the phone. I'll be down to see you." So he came down. He came down to see me on Greenpoint Avenue, and with Celentano was Frisher and Gallagher.

Q. All right, where did you go to?

A. Over the Greenpoint Avenue Bridge, by the cemetery.

Q. In one car?

A. No, I went in my car, they went in their car.

Q. All right. When you got to the cemetery, what happened?

A. Well, Pete got out of his car and said, "Don't say nothing in front of Frisher."

Q. Say nothing about what?

A. The Babe Dereda thing.

Q. Did he say why?

A. Frisher was not there.

Q. *Frisher was not in on that?*

A. *No, Frisher was not in on that.*

Q. *And then what happened?*

A. *Well, he asked me—*

Q. *(Interrupting) Then did you remain outside the car or did you go in the car?*

A. *No, we got in the car.*

Q. *And what was said in the car?*

A. *He asked me what I was doing and I told him I wasn't doing anything, and because he was brought into the office and asked about me…And he told me not to do anything, he didn't want to hear from me, "Just lay low." I was hot. And, "Get lost."*

SLOUCHING FROM BROOKLYN

When I wrote *Subway to California*, I had an incomplete picture of my family. Of course, I still do and perhaps to some extent always will. I still have an incomplete picture of myself. But I knew I didn't have all the pieces in place, and that was my burden to read between the lines, make a few guesses. My father never held dinner company spellbound by his stories. There was never much in the way of company around, at dinner or any other hour, and nobody touted him as the Italian Frank McCourt. Yet my hunches, based upon my father's rare and truncated and oblique disclosures, were occasionally in the ballpark, as it turned out.

The details surfaced unexpectedly and fleshed out the history when I lurched upon the transcripts of three of my father's trials that Google posted in January 2015. Google may be richly deserving of the privacy- and copyright-protection criticism leveled against it, but these materials were a godsend. I am neither a consumer advocate nor a legal scholar, but I know what I like. And no amicus briefs in support of the tech giant will be forthcoming from me. I have written some books, however, and I taught for a long time, and I had my own dustup with the FBI when I was a young man, so I could read the testimony and I had a personal stake in the findings. Nobody in my family besides me ever graduated from high school, and there were no book discussions or bedtime readings in my Greenpoint home, but I think it's probably not the worst upbringing to grow up with a father who was a criminal and a snitch, a fabricator and a world-class evader who internalized the street maxim that nobody was ever hanged for something he didn't say, and he didn't say much—at least before those trials. Probably not terrible DNA for a novelist, poet, and memoirist.

This book of mine begins with an assertion: I am not my father.

And with a question: how would I know one way or the other?

THE POPE MEETS SANTA

Q. You knew that when you gave that answer, you were telling an untruth,
* didn't you?*

A. No, I wasn't lying about it. You didn't give me a chance.

Except for a few newspaper articles and my refracted childhood recollections, most knowable information about his criminal life is gleaned from police disciplinary proceedings that took place in Manhattan, 1961–62, and as recorded in *New York State Appellate Division, Records and Briefs*:

1949

Convicted of bookmaking in Brooklyn, given a suspended sentence, pays a fine of twenty-five or fifty dollars (evidence varies). Testified twelve years later that he took the arrest for a bookmaker named Jim Discano as a favor, which was known as a "stand-in" arrest.

He is twenty years old, residing in Brooklyn, though he sometimes gives his address as my grandparents' farm in East Islip. I am born in 1950; my brother John, fifteen months later, in 1951; my parents marry at St. Cecilia's Catholic Church in Greenpoint on February 21, 1953. That means that for at least a few years my mom is a single, unmarried, and divorced young woman living with her four sons (John and me, along with my two older half-brothers, Bobby and Eddie, share one bedroom) in her working-class, Catholic, Polish, and Italian 'hood of Greenpoint. Her living arrangement might have conceivably tested a woman possessed of less intestinal fortitude. She was evidently immune to any social stigma. This observation would not shock anybody who was her neighbor, waiter, physician, priest, spouse, or offspring.

My father moves into my mother's apartment around the time of their wedding; before then, he would visit his two boys, he told me in his advanced years, take them in a carriage to the park a couple of blocks away. This is her second and last marriage; his one and only. If anybody snapped wedding portraits, I never saw them framed on the mantle (no mantles either). And if they ever once in their long married lives celebrated their wedding anniversary, I missed the festivities. As for the date of his wedding, he testified that he was married, not in 1953, but in 1948. Husbands can be confused on the anniversary subject, or so I have been curtly informed on occasion, but that seems a significant alteration of the timeline. It's probably a reach to make too much of this. After all, he was attention-challenged and, at the moment he offered that misinformation, battling with a pit bull attorney.

1950

Convicted of petty larceny in the Bronx (theft of granite monuments). Pleads guilty, receives a suspended sentence.

1955-57

Jobless. Operates as a paid confidential informant for Officer Vincent "Jimmy" Santa, whom he knew from the neighborhood, who is stationed in Brooklyn. His information, he believed and contended, led to many arrests.

Meets Officer John Tartarian and Officer John Scire through Santa. Under oath, Tartarian later denies knowing him.

FEBRUARY 1957

Fingers bookmaker Sal Valenti, mentioned before; Officers John Tartarian and Baldasaro "Benny" Ficalora shake down Valenti for six hundred dollars. Receives one hundred dollars from Tartarian later that night.

DECEMBER 23, 1960

Unemployed again; laid off as stonecutter.

Testifies that he owed loan sharks $1,500 and was in debt for a total of about $3,000; most of the money used by him to gamble. States that gambling was not his business, it was his "vice."

JANUARY 29, 1961

Playing cards with Joe Cacavella, "Babe" Dareda, and Junior Loterzio. Picks up a name and number for a possible score. Tells Santa; Santa and Officer Peter Celentano "hit" the location in Maspeth, but nothing there.

(Hallmark Opportunity: this is his wife's birthday.)

FEBRUARY 20, 1961

Celentano calls, informs my father his phone is tapped.

Meets with Celentano and Officer John Gallagher; they want a name of a bookmaker they can shake down. Owes Celentano $150-$200. Gives them a name: Corky, but that revelation does not bear fruit. Celentano wants more names. Gives him the names and license plate numbers of two other bookmakers: Dominick Spinelli and Joe Cacavella.

MARCH 1961

Informed by Santa his phone is tapped.

LATE MARCH 1961

Meets with Celentano, Santa, Gallagher, and Officer David Frisher; waits with them in a truck and then points out a bookmaker. The cops score "Cock-eyed Jerry" for $1,000.

Receives one hundred dollars, his cut, from Santa the next week.

Provides Santa with another name, a bookmaker on parole, "Babe" Dereda. Cops go to Dereda's house, score $2,000. Receives $250 from Celentano, who also forgives a debt of $125. Celentano tells him they should "start from scratch," an apparent reference to the forgiven loan.

Targets Junior Loterzio as another potential score during that meeting with Celentano. Celentano tells him they should let things cool down for now after the two recent scores totaling $3,000.

APRIL 12, 1961

Santa dismissed from the police force after he refuses to answer questions pertaining to Di Prisco and presumably about the shakedowns of "Cock-eyed" Jerry and Dereda.

APRIL 15, 1961

Receives a call from Celentano, telling him not to say anything over the phone, prompting this writer to wonder all over again— what the hell was he was thinking, talking on the phone? Meets with Celentano, Gallagher, and Frisher on Greenpoint Avenue.

Later told by Celentano not to say anything about the Dereda score in front of Frisher because that cop wasn't in on it.

Also told by Celentano that he had been questioned by superiors about Di Prisco. Advised by Celentano to "lay low" and "get lost."

In testimony given six months later, he says that he never saw Celentano again after this meeting.

APRIL 18, 1961

Celentano questioned by high-ranking officers of the Police Commissioner's Confidential Investigations Unit (PCCIU); suspended for consorting with Di Prisco and another known gambler, Gerald "Cheesebox" Callahan, and for refusing to answer questions about them.

APRIL 19, 1961

The New York Times reports that Celentano and two other cops had been suspended for consorting with known criminals and gamblers, apparently a reference to Di Prisco and Callahan and others.

APRIL 20, 1961

The New York Times runs a follow-up story: "19 Police in Queens Shifted in Shake-up of Gambling Squad." Mentions suspension of Celentano and others.

LATE MAY/EARLY JUNE 1961

Law enforcement attempts to arrest my father at his parents' farm in East Islip, Long Island. He dashes into the woods and is not apprehended.

SUMMER 1961

Employed briefly in Massachusetts; drives to California.

My mother, younger brother, and I fly to San Francisco, where we meet my father sitting in his car at a gas station that was then located inside the airport. We live in a Santa Rosa motel for a while not to be confused with Hitchcock's famous *Psycho* setting, *eek eek eek eek eek*, and eventually arrive in Berkeley, where we take up residence. Berkeley? I know, right? Berkeley.

He finds work first as a stonecutter and later in a dairy.

JUNE 22, 1961

NYPD announces a big bust. Among the arrested are Officers Santa and Scire, along with Sebastian "Buster" Aloi and Dominick Spinelli, the bookmaker fingered by Di Prisco on February 20, 1961.

Aloi is reported to have extensive underworld ties, described as a capo with the Colombo crime family; reputedly a big-time mob loan shark.

Santa, Scire, and Aloi charged with extorting Spinelli by threatening to have him arrested in connection with a burglary ring that was responsible for more than $250,000 in hi-fi equipment thefts, if he did not pay them $2,000.

JULY 19, 1961

Di Prisco indictment filed in Queens for check forgery, grand larceny, and conspiracy. He is in California at the time. Bail is set at $2,500.

SEPTEMBER 26, 1961

Remains unclear as to whether or not he reached out to the NYPD or whether they found him. Unlawful flight, in legal parlance, carries with it a presumption of guilt. In any case, he waives extradition, is arrested in Berkeley by Lieutenant Walter Stone of the PCCIU, and returns to New York City. Testifies that he was in jail for five to seven days upon arriving.

I begin at Saint Joseph the Workman School in Berkeley.

SEPTEMBER 28, 1961

Arrested for forgery and grand larceny.

OCTOBER 1, 1961

Interrogated by the Police Commissioner's Confidential Investigations Unit, the forerunner of the Internal Affairs Bureau.

OCTOBER 4, 1961

Arrested on a warrant from Brooklyn for forgery.

OCTOBER 6, 1961

Questioned by PCCIU in connection with the February 1957 shakedown of the bookmaker Valenti. Officers Tartarian and Ahrens also questioned by PCCIU.

OCTOBER 18, 1961

Formally identifies Tartarian and Ficalora as the cops who did the Valenti shakedown.

OCTOBER 20, 1961

Provides testimony against Celentano; is the only witness in the departmental trial.

OCTOBER 27, 1961

Provides testimony against Tartarian and Ficalora pertaining to Valenti shakedown.

Discloses that there are charges awaiting him; says that he is "living in a hotel," where he was, according to the furiously exercised counsel for the accused, "treated like a pet."

He tells me, a year before he dies, that that was when he was being "squeezed" because he had "a lot of information."

Testifies that after he returned to New York City, the DA told him he "would be given consideration for [his] full cooperation."

FEBRUARY 8, 1962

Provides additional testimony with regard to Tartarian and Ficalora on the Valenti shakedown.

FEBRUARY 14, 1962

Court date in Queens on his indictments. Some kind of Valentine's Day.

APRIL 17, 1962

Celentano found guilty of consorting with gamblers and is dismissed from the NYPD. *The New York Times* reports that he had been linked with a paid informer, an apparent reference to Di Prisco.

APRIL 24, 1962

New York Herald Tribune: "Cop Fired for a Shakedown," referring to Celentano, who was convicted on the basis of Di Prisco's testimony on the shakedowns. Mentions that Celentano consorted with Di Prisco, who is identified by name as "a known criminal, gambler, and a person engaged in unlawful activities." Celentano is twenty-seven years old.

NOVEMBER 1962

Santa and Scire go on trial for attempted extortion of Spinelli; both plead guilty to a reduced charge of coercion. After Santa finishes his sentence and is back on the street, he becomes a full-fledged mobster.

JANUARY 16, 1963

Gallagher and Frisher found not guilty after departmental trial.

Police commissioner states that Di Prisco's testimony during their trial is unworthy of belief.

MAY 16, 1963

Tartarian and Ficalora formally dismissed in connection with the Valenti shakedown.

1963

My father has a job. He wears white coveralls with *Joe* stitched in red scripted thread on his chest, and drives a truck for a dairy in Oakland, California. I am twelve and he is thirty-eight years old.

NEW YORK STATE APPELLATE DIVISION

RECORDS AND BRIEFS

Q. *All right, now that your answer then was incorrect, is that right, is that right, was it right, or was it wrong?*

A. *I seen money in the envelope.*

Q. *So that—if you said—*

A. *(Interrupting) I'm not going to say incorrect, I seen money in the envelope.*

Q. *If this answer, which it appears on the record when you—*

A. *(Interrupting) I'm not going to say—*

Q. *(Interrupting) Just a minute. You said you didn't see any money, that answer was incorrect?*

A. *I seen money in the envelope. I'm not going to say I didn't see it.*

Q. *Well, you just said you might have said it.*

A. *At the time, I might have said it, but there was money in the envelope.*

DOG IN THE RAIN

My parents were in their sixties, it was Christmas Eve, and Patti, my wife, and I decked the halls of our Berkeley home, *fa la la la la, la la la la*. We put on dinner for the ragtag family bunch. The twinkling tree, carols playing, the prime rib and the Yorkshire pudding, the exchange of gifts, dogs stretched out before the hearth: the whole traditional festive nine yards that was never quite the yardage tradition in this family. My mother often liked to mix it up with me and others around holidays and birthdays and formal occasions. A solid percentage of time, she and I weren't talking when those dates rolled around. Although she never missed off-to-prison or welcome-home-from-prison parties, when and where she arrived with her world-class cheesecake or cream puffs, she famously elected, for reasons never elucidated, not to attend my one and only wedding celebration. On this Christmas, she showed and gave out some nice presents, as I recall, and in general became progressively more accomplished at gift-giving, and more generous, the older she got. In the aftermath of this not quite silent night, I thought the dinner went all right, but I always tempered hopes and reserved summary judgment.

I never could predict where my parents would take it the next day, what imagined slights they had managed to absorb, although it might be impossible for them to articulate. So I called up, Christmas Day, to check in on their mood, to see what they were up to, prepared to take my medicine if it came to that. The old man was depressed. He didn't use the word, which wasn't in his working vocabulary, but he didn't have to.

"Went out, looked for Chinese," he said, pronouncing it "Chineese." In his most miserable tone of voice he added: "Like a dog in the rain."

He liked his egg rolls and wonton soup, but I would never underestimate his gargantuan appetite for disappointment. I might characterize this disposition as self-pity, but that doesn't seem quite on the mark. Nothing seemed more obvious than that he had suffered in the remote past some deep primal wound. He would not be healed. As with my mother, my father continually conveyed the sense that he was being left out. It was hard to miss their conveying the suspicion that if they were attending some social gathering, say Christmas Eve dinner, they knew there was a better one from which they had been excluded.

If the wine tasted good, they could have been served better—by somebody who appreciated them better. It was a foolproof formula. Their congenital disillusionment contaminated the atmosphere: I had not done enough for them. I don't doubt that they were sincere when they felt like dogs in the rain, either. It didn't even have to be raining.

In his eighties my father once confided to his brilliant and kind care manager, who ultimately became a friend of mine, "I have lots of problems." She tried to draw him out, so that he might expand upon what he meant, she reported, but all he came up with was, "I'm not too good at finding solutions."

My old school unschooled father never heard of Montaigne and nobody would ever be reminded of that melancholic French luminary of the Renaissance, but maybe somebody should be. It is irresistible to quote the author of classic personal essays when he writes, "If my mind could gain a firm footing I would not make essays, I would make decisions."

Testimony

About my parents' formal education: neither of them completed high school, if they attended at all; they never spun stories about the big game and the prom and student body elections, that's for sure. My mother was the youngest of nine children born to her immigrant, Warsaw-born parents. She became pregnant at sixteen, married her first husband, and although she was exceptionally intelligent, going to school probably constituted a lost cause. But she and my father did send me and my brother to Catholic schools in Brooklyn and later in California. The financial cost must have stressed the budget, because they were hardly rolling in it. I have to presume, therefore, that they assigned some sort of high value to our education and deemed it worth the sacrifice. They kept my grade school report cards in shoe boxes and attended all my commencement exercises, including from graduate school at Berkeley. At the same time they conveyed ambivalence if not skepticism as to the virtues or advantages of being educated. *Don't be fucking smart*, I heard all the time when I was perceived to have acted up. I enjoyed all the advantages of being the resident outsider, not an unpromising role for a writer in his youth to assume.

I probably unconsciously determined soon enough that the most effective way to revolt against my family was to be an anti-James Dean, a schoolboy, a rebel on the honor roll. My parents and my brother and my two half-brothers, my mother's sons from her previous marriage whom I looked up to, would, over time, have the other bases covered: rap sheets, gambling, drugs, reform school, prison, school dropouts. One of my half-brothers, Eddie, was closeted gay—and to be clear, I never thought of either of my half-brothers as half-anything, they were my *brothers*. His sexual status effectively rendered him an extreme outlier, at least in terms of our world, though everybody loved and admired him, touched by his kindness and generosity. Not that my parents directly acknowledged that he was gay, and they never voiced the word. No, toward the end of his life and even after, his partner of twenty years my mother called his roommate, somebody who to her way of thinking took advantage of the free rent—her terms. Once, after settling in California, I was stricken by guilt over my shoplifting career at a five-and-dime in Greenpoint. I must have been around eleven when I wrote Eddie a letter asking him to slip some money under the store door. I cannot recall if I sent him the cash, or if I assumed he would come out of pocket to alleviate my burden. I do know that years later he would tell me, laughing, that he never forgot Jo Jo's letter.

I would also be the devout little boy ambling down the street, off to Mass on Sunday by myself or with my little brother. Then when I was a teenager, I entered the novitiate of a Roman Catholic religious order, becoming for a while Brother Joseph, black robe, crucifix, and all. Later on I would have plenty of opportunity for my own battles with the law and drugs, and enduring money and career troubles of my own.

Shortly after I joined the order in pursuit of my vocation, and was installed in the Napa Valley novitiate, I was assigned a task: to clear out some of the heavy underbrush on the beautiful, secluded grounds of rolling vineyards. There were always chores: lavatory scrubbing, rug vacuuming, window washing, chapel cleanup, and so on. Good work to do. Good discipline, too.

On this occasion it was the middle of a sweltering summer day, and I took off my shirt and went to work, with resolve, on the unruly vegetation. I was an obedient novice, at that point, which could not always be said of me. Two problems occurred: I underestimated how swiftly and acutely my back and arms would burn beneath the Napa Valley skies, and I also didn't identify the poison oak I was blithely handling. Results were predictably terrible. That night, or the next day, my skin blistered and I found myself in my cell (that's what monasteries call individual rooms) hoping to die rather than to tolerate another minute. I would jump out the window into the vine rows below if it would give me momentary relief. In an attempt to distract myself (didn't get any lotions or drugs), and because I was probably too embarrassed to tell anybody what I had done, all I could do was sit on the edge of my cot and read. It was a James Bond novel. Books were always my go-to escape hatch. This time, no dice.

When my parents dropped me off that first Sunday afternoon to begin my stay at the Mount, they were taciturn as usual. Their clearest, most eloquent demonstration of emotion was revealed not through words, but as they drove down the hill away, when I could see my mother wiping her eyes. I had disappointed them again. And that was all right by me. I was seventeen and God was calling me to a life of poverty, chastity, and obedience, so I bellied up to the hallowed bar, for a while. I have no complaints about the Brothers and my spell being Brother Joseph in the novitiate. I mean, I did at the time, which is why I left, but when I look back, I realize this was never the life for me. Even so, I cherish the memories.

⌐

WINNICOTT MIGHT HAVE SOMETHING to contribute; he usually does. "For as children grow they like to copy their parents, or to defy them, which is just as good in the end" ("A Child's Sense of Right and Wrong"). Or:

"Finding the framework of his life broken, [the child] no longer feels free. He becomes anxious, and if he has hope he proceeds to look for a framework elsewhere than at home. The child whose home fails to give a feeling of security looks outside his home for the four walls; he still has hope, and he looks to grandparents, uncles and aunts, friends of the family, school. He seeks an external stability without which he may go mad." ("Aspects of Juvenile Delinquency.")

If you define yourself up against your family, that means your family continues to indirectly define you. So the anti-rebellious rebel label both does and does not quite fit me. I would not be pigeonholed a suck-up punk-ass poetry-writing pious pussy, even if I was as a matter of fact a suck-up punk-ass poetry-writing pious pussy. Likely because I was overcompensating, I managed to be suspended from all the schools I attended (hooky, fisticuffs, major crimes of that order). One upstate New York wintry dawn, I came to be expelled by the president of my university. That's what happened when I was one of the anti-war-protesting leaders of the college admin building takeover; he eventually rescinded that decision because he was a magnanimous and Machiavellian fellow who ran circles around us sleep-deprived, snow-booted, ponytailed radicals. In general I never had trouble succeeding academically. I had a lot of trouble feeling that getting good grades was ever good enough, ever exciting enough.

As for defining myself up against my family, here is one glaring problem: I believe I never quite grasped the very notion of family, or harbored some conception of an ideal family or, for that matter, a so-called normal family. This also sounds strange to me, too, but I didn't get it. It was the sound of one hand clapping. As one of the first great psychologists of child development, Harry Stack Sullivan, proposed long ago: the principal adolescent project is the avoidance of loneliness and the pursuit of the impossible-to-define normal. My fragmented, contentious family bestowed upon me a fractured sense of what a family is, or could be. I may have been a father at twenty-five but I didn't marry till I was forty-one, and that wasn't to my son's mother. I consciously set out at that late stage catching up on making a family, whatever that could mean, and I am still making up for lost time and opportunity. I've been married twenty-five years now, and my wife and my son have both taught me through their open-hearted example what family could be.

〰

As MY FATHER SAID that time to his caremanager, *"I have lots of problems."* His statement sounds somewhat self-reflective, if not quite philosophical. In that encompassing sense, these are the words of a man I never knew or spoke to in his lifetime.

Whenever with reference to my father I write "testify" or "testimony," I automatically summon up Saint Augustine, whose *Confessions* has long been one of the central texts of my life. I hold Garry Wills accountable for this strange tic of mine. In his short, trenchant book *Saint Augustine*, Wills explains that *Confessions* is not quite the correct title. He proposes that the more accurate title is *The Testimony*. He isn't making an academic argument or a purely etymological distinction, either. The name change doesn't look as if it will stick in the public consciousness anytime soon, but maybe Wills will win the day eventually. For as he argues, *Confessions* implies more than what we take to be "confessions." It also implies praise of God and profession of faith. In this sense, it means to corroborate, to confirm, to acknowledge, so that even inanimate things can *testify*:

> Augustine was not confessing like an Al Capone, or like a pious trafficker of later confessions. In fact, his use of the term is so broad, one can ask why he bothers to insist that he *is* testifying, since everything, whether it knows it or not, testifies to God. Even demons "confess" (acknowledge) God by their opposition to him.

For Augustine, when "the tongue and the heart are at odds, you are reciting, not testifying." Augustine's book is autobiography and the prayerful meditation of a once-upon-a-time spectacular debauchee and libertine reclaiming his life for God, a work famous and influential not solely because he wrote, "God, give me chastity, but not now." Still, what a handy little prayer under proper, or not so much, circumstances.

In a much-discussed moment in his autobiography, Augustine tells about the time as a boy he raided an orchard and stole pears.

He makes a great deal of the fact that the pears were not beautiful or delicious and that he and a "band of ruffians" took the pears "not to eat them ourselves, but to throw them to the pigs. Perhaps we ate some of them, but our real pleasure consisted in doing something that was forbidden." It's a primal and complex life-changing moment for him. Among other things, he says that he knows he wouldn't have committed this wanton act if he were alone, but he did so because he was with the others. His love was not so much for the pears as for his companionship of his peers. He draws conclusions about the right relationship to God, the twisted path he was following, but Wills makes a connection between the fruit and Augustine's analysis of Adam and Eve in the Garden of Eden, in his *City of God*. Eve falls for the serpent's lies, writes Wills, but Adam is the less deceived: "Adam committed his sin deliberately in order to maintain his 'bond of company' with Eve." As Augustine explains:

> After Eve had eaten from the forbidden tree and offered him its fruit to eat along with her, Adam did not want to disappoint her, when he thought she might be blighted without his comforting support, banished from his heart to die sundered from him.

By this reading, Adam discards paradise and the promise of eternal bliss—here comes the bombshell—so as not to disappoint his wife and because he could not bear to live without her. He might have been the first but he would not be the last spouse to enact this strategy. Though my father could conceive of his and his wife's banishing themselves from Brooklyn, obviously no Eden, he could not tolerate, for all of the never-ending marital warfare, the possibility of his wife's banishment from his life. And she undoubtedly would have concurred. Throughout my childhood, and beyond, she railed against him and threatened divorce. It was upsetting to hear her denunciations, but on another level I could tell she was bluffing. As they say in poker, don't call unless you are prepared to raise.

For the truth is, my parents were in psychological terms absolutely *enmeshed*, which was the diagnosis of his geriatric psychologist caremanager. That is, these were two people so closely intertwined as to be unable to determine where one of them ended and the other began. There is no better way to conceptualize what held them together in their bonds of mutual misery for almost sixty years other than that they could not envision an alternative. The trite term *codependent* barely scratches the surface, it is much too cautious. Their connection was more visceral and violent than that. They survived on the same oxygen; when one exhaled, the other breathed in. They tenaciously held on to the opposite ends of the same rope. As Augustine writes in summation about his desecration of the orchard: "Can anyone unravel this twisted tangle of knots?"

Divided Selves

I confidently hypothesize that, if my father never explicitly addressed the allure of the criminal life, he glamorized it. If he didn't, he would have been different from everybody else in the neighborhood.

For instance, all of us kids knew of the hit man who lived on the block. He had a name, but it's lost to me. He resided five or so houses down from mine, and the whole world would come to a spooky standstill when he opened his door and hawkishly surveyed the street, left and right, for a moment. On the lookout for drive-by shooters? No idea. We fell into a hush and studied him at a safe distance as he walked down the steps of his stoop, slow as destiny, ponderous as inevitability. He was a huge and meaty guy, with arms like legs, and legs like tree trunks. His puffed, pallid face was absolutely expressionless, as we imagined to be the requisite mien of conscienceless killers. He moved with a graceless purposefulness, wasting no effort, again as we imagined to be consistent with a hit man's remorseless efficiency. From a distance he appeared ageless, but I feared making eye contact, which might lead to unpleasant consequences. He never acknowledged punks like us or uttered a single word in our direction. We observed him when he was leaving his apartment, which means we only saw him at dusk, the hour we must have concluded that killers punch in for work. We were in awe. He was one of us and deadly. He even lived with his mother. Not that anybody ever saw her. My brother Bobby, who feared nobody and was a pretty tough guy himself, signaled this was nobody to mess with. When we trick-or-treated on Halloween, nobody'd be crazy enough to knock on that guy's door. How'd we determine he was a hit man? This is stuff you simply know when you're a Brooklyn kid. He didn't scrawl HIT MAN where his name should have been beside the doorbell, which, again, you'd be out of your mind to think of ringing.

Was he in reality a hired assassin? Odds would be against his sporting such a CV, I suppose, but I have no idea. In our boyhood conception of mythologized reality, he cut a menacing figure, and of that I am as sure as I am of anything. He never amounted to our version of Boo Radley, Harper Lee's recluse and the vessel of Scout's childhood mystery, the familiar stranger who materializes to reclaim innocence and goodness for the town. Yeah, on every single level, that wouldn't have sufficed for us. And maybe he was nothing but a big fat mama's boy who had no life and washed dishes at an all-night diner. Nobody was going to tug on his coat sleeve or trail him to find out.

Then there was my mother's best friend who lived in the nicest house by far on the block. She had a boyfriend who favored flashy clothes, such as red blazers and black shirts, and he drove a white Caddy, and his face was so crimson that I assumed he was holding his breath—either that or he was drunk again. Nice guy, but we gave him wide berth, too. Rumor was he was a mobster. My dad indicated he was unimpressed by the man, and *that* position impressed me. (Curiously, this fellow, Mike Gallo, appears in cameo in one trial transcript, the partner of a bookmaker my father fingered and the dirty cops popped.)

When I think of my dad's past, I may, of course, be romanticizing him, or myself. I may not be in the past at all. As Augustine proposes: "If we could suppose some particle of time which could not be divided into a smaller particle, that alone deserves to be called the present, yet it is snatched from the future and flits into the past without any slightest time of its own—if it lasted, it could be divided into part-future and part-past. So there is no 'present' as such."

"And yet," Wills glosses, "we know that past only as a *present memory* and the future only as a *present* anticipation. There is, then, no real present and nothing *but* a real present. The mind brokers this odd interplay of times in a no-time."

That's where and when I find myself here and now: in this "no-time."

⁓

DID MY FATHER HAVE internal crises? A crisis of consciousness? Ever? Did he have an internal life? Who doesn't? That last one is not a rhetorical question.

On this score, I summon up an odd, somewhat trivial image pertaining to me and him. Once he took me to the San Francisco airport when I was heading back to college. On the way to the departure gate (back when you could do that), we ventured into the bookstore, and he bought me something to read for the trip, a skinny hardback I badly wanted. This was a famous book by probably the most controversial psychologist of the day. The author published it when he was thirty-three and an international celebrity, and it treated the subject of schizophrenia, not that I shared this intel with my father, who merely wanted to do something nice for me about to board a red-eye bound for New York. As I view it now, the book adopted a psychologically questionable approach, if not morally bankrupt, and not that I saw it that way when I was in college; that was when I looked for every opportunity to name-drop the author in footnotes to my papers about anything, poetry, history, politics, *anything*. I think it's fair to argue that the author essentially valorized schizophrenia, viewed it as a species of liberation from convention, and as a result he clinically failed patients, who needed not fancy cheap psychedelicized theorization but medical care and treatment. It is a wildly irresponsible book, finally, but when I was in college this point of view entranced me, feeling unbalanced as I did at the time, and feeling split within myself all day long. The author was R. D. Laing, whose star has probably permanently sunk, and the book my unsuspecting father gave to me was *The Divided Self*.

Star Witness

A few years ago, I attended the memorial of a school friend. He had become an undercover cop in a rough part of the Bay Area, and he had made his rep by infiltrating the Hells Angels. We had talked about his experience a few times over the years. It was clear he didn't escape without paying a serious psychic price. Big, tough guy, but a sweet man, and a beloved dad, too. I always liked Carlos. He died after an extended bout of excruciating physical suffering.

His older brother approached us, school alums gathered together reminiscing about our old classmate. He thanked us for being there, many of whom he hadn't seen for forty years.

"Rich," somebody said to him, gesturing toward me, "you remember Joe Di Prisco?"

He studied me. "I sure do. But who's this guy?"

SO OF COURSE, WE may change, by choice or by chance, and sometimes it isn't pretty. I conceive of my own life as having an arc or two or three, along with a swoop and a crash and a whoosh or two—or ten. How come my father's life didn't? I can only conjecture. Am I striving to think in terms of what I presume to be his fixed ideas, or am I assigning to him my fixed ideas and preoccupations about him? And what if I flipped the basic storyline? Instead of his being a small-time criminal who cleaned up his act and went (comparatively) straight in his late-thirties—what if he, as a teenager and a young man, made some mistakes that endangered him and put him in hot water, from which he eventually extricated himself, transforming himself into a solid citizen in the process?

Good guy, bad guy. Sinner, saint. Hood, hero. Scammer, searcher. All simplistic paradigms. Nobody's life can be usefully viewed in black and white. And experience is not linear. More like circular, or parabolic.

I could have a tiny clue as to a possible life-changing moment he experienced in 1961. Being cross-examined, he is asked about how he came to remember precise, crucial details as to a crime he alleged to have witnessed.

A. *I just came back from California.*

Q. *Anything in California to refresh the memory?*

A. *I left the family behind.*

Q. *Now, how does it refresh the memory?*

A. *At the time it did.*

∽

COULD IT BE THAT he finally registered, long after the deeds he committed, how much he had jeopardized himself when he engaged in his criminal activities? Is it possible that for conceivably the first time in his life he was grasping how much he was going to lose—or how much he had already lost—namely, his freedom and his family, whatever that was, whatever it meant to him? And did this recognition dawn upon him once he was "safe" in California and therefore in greatest danger of seeing himself as he truly was?

In the moment of being on the stand, when he curiously and awkwardly reached for a different narrative link to explain the functions of his mind and the acts of his will, was he attempting to conceptualize his life as a series of disastrous choices that might be rectified? Perhaps unconsciously, was he framing his decision to appear in court as a type of affirmation of some value or principle beyond himself?

A. *I left the family behind.*

Q. *Now, how does it refresh the memory?*

A. *At the time it did.*

There is a chance he was making a play for sympathy, as a dad and a husband seeking reclamation and rehabilitation, and that possibility should not be gainsaid. But equally likely, to me, there stood a chance while testifying that he was caught in the act of actively fashioning meaning, fresh meaning in what had thus far been the senseless catastrophe of a young man's life. It would have been easy, for instance, to see the futility of his flight from justice, but that is precisely what he resisted. This recognition, if real, would relate to his bookmaking and playing the horses. Nothing feels emptier than the vacancy of gambling and losing. And as for his small-time criminal life, at some juncture at least he must have seen how utterly pointless that all was. Not that he possessed the language to express this thought, but Popey never gave in to the siren call of nihilism. If anything, he might have viewed himself as a type of hero questing for something beyond himself: *I left the family behind and I'm trying to do right now.* More than anything, *I am not a victim, I am willing a free choice.* Self-serving? Who knows, but judgers gonna judge anyway.

Similarly, when the cross-examining lawyer pressed him elsewhere by asking if he gambled for a living, my father adamantly disputed the accusation:

Q: *You didn't tell him, "I'm working as a stonecutter, but I'm really a big gambler," did you?*

A: *Well, he knew I gambled.*

Q: *Well, was that your business?*

A: *No, it was a vice.*

Q: *It was a vice? You put bets on horses, is that it?*

A: *Yes, sir.*

Q: *You went to the track?*

A: *Well, I went to the track and bet with bookmakers.*

Q: *Is that all you do, bet on horses? Is that your specialty, your vice?*

A: *Gambler.*

Being a gambler, he said in effect, was not a career choice; his gambling was, in essence, his "vice." That is, he declined to view his gambling as a failed profit-seeking business venture. On numerous other occasions at home, during those knockdown drag-outs with my mom, he heard her call him a fucking degenerate, but the charge stiffened his spine, and he didn't buy that label, either. As he states above for the record, he viewed his gambling as a moral failing and his falling. Admittedly, his singularly ready frame of reference for a defect on this order was not philosophy or medical diagnosis or mental disorder. If anything, the context for admission of vice was something like morality, or at least some pale sense of religiosity. His gambling might have been incurable, he couldn't take a pill for that. And yet, maybe he was merely bullshitting, and it wouldn't be the first time if he were. His language suggests his conceivable, diffuse awareness of an overarching ethical spectrum. And though he was no moral theologian or ethicist, a man named Popey who owned up in public to personal degradation might feel not blame so much as guilt. I don't want to overstate this case, but maybe I am doing so anyway. A man who calls his gambling compulsion a vice also might catch sight of a hopeful glimmering of the flip side of the damnation caused by his wickedness: salvation. Again, did this move constitute an implicit, calculated appeal for sympathy? After all, who among us is not a sinner? he might have added. Then again, in the company of cops and criminals, he didn't need to.

〜

THE OLDER AND FRAILER he got, the more helpless and the more dependent he begrudgingly became. His one-word routinely invoked mantra was *family*. This was understandable, and strategic. In his burgeoning anger and flickering dementia, he swung it like a truncheon to urge me to pay attention to him. It sounded like a foreign language, and I did my best to speak it.

Am I conducting a sort of dialogue with my deceased parents? And to what end at this point in my life? But wait. Do we ever stop conducting conversations with the dead? And the *dead*? Are they truly, absolutely dead? Maybe they in some sense exist in the present because there is nothing but a present time for them—in our imagination.

NEW YORK STATE APPELLATE DIVISION

RECORDS AND BRIEFS

Q. Did you ever try to set up a man by the name of Junior Loturicio?

A. I don't—I didn't.

Q. Do you know what I mean by the word "set up," do you know?

A. You can explain it to me.

Q. Do you know what I mean?

A. No, sir. You explain it.

Q. You are a professional informer—weren't you?

A. What do you mean, "professional"?

Q. Do you know what an informer is?

A. Yes, but what do you mean, "professional"?

Q. Got paid?

A. Got paid for the information?

Q. Got paid for informing—did you ever inform on a man by the name of Junior Loturicio?

A. No.

Q. Did you ever suggest that you had information about Junior Loturicio?

A. Yes.

CUTTING STONE

I do not know how much schooling my father had, but it couldn't have been a lot. Given that he was cannot-sit-still, jumpy-as-a-cat, I can imagine that for a youngster like him sitting in a desk would be unalloyed torture. So then, what is an uneducated, first-generation Italian American like him, fresh out of the service in WWII, supposed to do to make a living in Brooklyn in the 1940s and '50s? In his case, he works as a runner for a bookmaker and also a numbers operator; in 1947, he's twenty-two, and he takes the pinch for the book when he is arrested. The judge sees through the young man's guilty plea and dismisses the charges—or so my father told me.

My dad and I used to talk in his assisted living apartment in California, a few miles from my home. At this time, he and I were spending the most time together since my earliest childhood. He required round-the-clock care, and his residence was a sophisticated, kindly operation. By then, he had lost interest in television, including sports, absolutely stymied by the challenge of the remote control. He would soon to be on his way to the euphemistically named memory wing for the seriously demented, from which he bailed almost immediately because he detested the joint, as well as the company of sad droolers and drifters and specialists of the non sequitur. One day, he was in a semi-garrulous mood with me, so I took the opportunity to ask him if he had ever been arrested. At the time, I didn't know.

"No," he said.

Count to three. One, two…

"Once."

Yeah, that's my old man.

Records indicate that he was convicted on that 1947 occasion, given a suspended sentence. I do think it is possible he may have been confused, believing *suspended* meant *dismissed*. Beyond that, as I would come to discover from a rap sheet and other trial proceedings, he was actually arrested at least five times in his life.

∽

ALONG WITH "DON'T GET involved," "keep it to yourself" was another catchphrase of his, his response to anybody ever giving up inside, that is, emotional information, or venturing a report from the hinterland of feelings. Like the time my brother John, briefly in recovery, told him across a Thanksgiving table that he loved him. My father instantaneously countered: "Yeah, well, keep it to yourself." Such displays of vulnerability must have struck him as being unmanly if not "embarrassing," a prime term in his rhetorical arsenal. His most potent threat to me when I misbehaved as a child: "I'm gonna embarrass you." Consistent with his lifelong commitment to keep things to himself, he said he never told his wife about that first conviction—information that came out in a much later case when he gave sworn testimony. That arrest took place before she divorced her first husband, yet I doubt she was in the dark. She didn't miss much of anything until she started missing everything on account of her own Alzheimer's.

In general, he was not susceptible to the appeal of TMI. That was the prime reason my son and I were never really worried about a stranger scamming him when he was losing it. If some lowlife scum crooks on the phone tried to get him to give up his social security number and credit card, which they did indeed try to do, in the end he'd be more likely to get theirs. The last real argument Mario and I had took place when I appropriated my father's credit cards. My son was indignant, complained that I was undercutting his grandfather's self-respect, and contended there was no real downside to his keeping or using the credit cards. What's the worst that could happen, if, say, he blew some money on something or other? To me it wasn't about the cash burn, and I lost my temper, but after calming down, I did arrange for my father's personal caremanager to go over with the grandson all the risks, which she contended were considerable, given his impaired mental capacity and his tendency to outfox his handlers and his proclivity to ramble away from the security of his residence when the handler's attention wavered. That conversation, along with some books I gave him about Alzheimer's insidious pathways, helped Mario change his tune and come around, though my father never did. He was furious. Furious until, finally, he lost that edge, too. But I should underscore that all of us were struggling to understand how to deal with him and his dementia. He had entered that twilight, upside-down, Alice-in-Wonderland, surreal realm, and we were all on the fast track to incomprehension and frustration.

As for his liquid assets, when he was in assisted living, he seemed to be rolling in cash. His care manager told me she had never had a client who threw around money like him, somebody who seemingly had thousands of dollars handy. He had a penchant for trying to tip out the staff. Employees' accepting gratuities was strictly forbidden, but I don't think house rules stopped him or dissuaded them. I can't help but imagine that, for an old Teamster boss like him, he might have enjoyed the unionized fantasy of organizing the help. Once I took advantage of his having a dental appointment and searched his apartment. I went through everything and uncovered no stash of cash. He still had his chops. And he had more surprises up his sleeve—and in his pockets. Without prompting or a word of explanation, he one day transformed into an ATM before my very eyes. He reached into his right pants pocket, pulled out a roll of hundreds, and handed it to me. Good, I thought, maybe my message had gotten through to him, and maybe he was trusting me, and maybe he was giving over to an acceptance of his state. I told him I would put away the money for safekeeping. Then in a minute he reached into his left pants pocket and pulled out another roll of hundreds. And then a little while later, he reached into his back pants pocket and—yet another roll. I must have asked if that was it, and he must have indicated it was. I didn't exactly believe him, because why start now, but I was yet again impressed.

〜

DURING THE WAR, HE enlisted at sixteen in the Coast Guard and shipped out on a troop transport in the Atlantic, where he served as a fireman in the engine room. That sounded scary. But he also said he ran the dice games on the ship. When I asked him about how he managed that, he said he stole what he could. (Maybe not so coincidentally, my brother ran blackjack games in prison, where he took the unsuspecting players for everything he could—more about this, and John, soon.) Eventually my dad was honorably discharged, and late into his life he marched in war vet parades and wore pins on his lapels and proudly flew the American flag from his porch on patriotic holidays.

When he landed in Naples, he said, he and some fellow sailors fell in with some locals who offered up their sister for their pleasure, and for the brothers' profit. It seems the guys threw their money on the table, but then got cold feet. "It wasn't right," my dad said. He also said he stole some food from the ship and gave it to the impoverished Italians, who obviously needed help. He liked the ladies his whole life, and they reciprocated, but if he ever cheated on his wife (who probably cheated on him, if reports and my recollections are real), he never tipped his hand. He had a courtly, somewhat prudish, side. Once we all went up to Reno where we submitted ourselves to an inane casino show. The comic was performing a very blue act, and my father looked abundantly offended, if not nauseated. It took all his self-control not to run out of the place.

Then there was a time we hired a professional companion to spend a few hours with him in his assisted living; this is fairly standard practice. We thought it would be beneficial for him to not be alone for long stretches, to talk with another person who was proficient at dealing with the elderly and demented. In short order, he dismissed her. He explained to the incredulous supervisor that the woman wanted to have sex with him, and he was upset. He reminded her he was a married man. That was when my mother had been dead for two years.

As a young man home from the war in 1945, he took jobs at various times in a dairy and most prominently as a stonecutter, following in the steps of my naturalized-citizen grandfather who brought the trade with him from Fontanarosa, a picturesque but economically depressed mining village a couple of hours outside Naples.

A few years ago, Patti and I made an excursion to the town. I wanted to see what family records were accessible. The functionary on duty at first didn't appear pleased to be of service, insofar as the sacrosanct lunch hour beckoned. But our Italian was in good shape, and before long, she relented cheerfully. She came up with my grandparents' wedding papers and birth certificates. At some point, the postal delivery woman stopped in, nosy about the visitors, and made conversation; Americans in town, maybe this could be diverting. I asked her, in Italian, if there were any Di Priscos nearby. She rolled her eyes and threw up her hands and indicated the place was crawling with them. I didn't look anybody up.

As for stonecutting, it's hard to imagine more strenuous, backbreaking, potentially injurious labor. I recollect one day being in a car picking up my nonno and dad from the stonecutter's, and I can picture the coating of gray dust all over them and the blue rags they wiped their faces with. My father is eventually fired by this employer, and is arrested for pilfering stone from the shop. His rap sheet itemizes the arrest but gives no details as to the case's disposition, but in testimony given during the dirty-cop trials he owns up to the larceny.

Mostly, he bet the horses, thoroughbreds or trotters, whatever was in season. And therefore he was always looking for money, because he was not cleaning up at the track. He was a good handicapper, I would come to realize, but even good handicappers are not good enough to keep in the black. As one cop, later dismissed from the force, said in his testimony about him, "This man is in dire need of money at all times. He'd ask anybody, he'd give up his mother for money."

"Fast" Eddie Felson in *The Color of Money* says: "Money won is twice as sweet as money earned." That's from Richard Price's screenplay, and, as with most things, he hits it out of the park. Nobody ever bothered to say that money lost is aromatic as cigar ashes, or that the memory of the occasional win ever counterbalances memories of the bad beats.

HERE IS AS GOOD a place as any to disclose that there was a time when I did business with bookmakers of my own, when I put money down on games and races in the premobile-phone era, including when I was an English graduate student instructor at Berkeley, where there was a convenient pay phone (remember pay phones?) outside my Wheeler Hall classroom and from which I could make, if so inclined, a bet or two during class breaks. Was I a gambler, did I have my old man's vice? I was traveling in social circles, excuse the term, of guys who carried crisp stacks of cash in their Italian leather purses and bet very serious money, guys who knew stuff, smart guys, wise guys. I learned from them. This was a different sort of liberal education for a schoolboy like me. I never bet the favorite in my life, rule one of many good rules. Did I go broke? Not right away. Did I buy a house in Beverly Hills? Also no. Did I borrow from loan sharks? I wasn't that irrational. I had other vices I preferred.

I also played blackjack professionally for high stakes around the world for several years, in my late twenties and early thirties, bankrolled by big-money backers who recruited me when I worked as a waiter in one of their restaurants. I never considered that gambling, even while I was playing hands where thousands of dollars rode on the turn of the next card. To my mind and more importantly to the mind of my backers, I was adept in doing on-the-fly statistical probability analysis—that is, I counted cards in blackjack in numerous casinos in Vegas, Reno, the Caribbean, South Africa, Monte Carlo. I experienced it all. Offers to comp me Dom Perignon and call-girls. Big scores and equally big busts. Fast Eddie was right. Money won is indeed twice as sweet as money earned. I wish I had won more of it before I came to be barred, thanks to an international private detective agency, by what was then every casino in the world. But that is another story, told in *Subway*.

I would not allege I dabbled in the fine arts of wagering in order to gain a window into my dad's life, but it was something I acquired nonetheless. I knew what he thought about blackjack. He doggedly clung to crackpot strategies pertaining to hot decks and when to hit and when to stand and when to double down. All I recall is that everything he said was pretty much dead wrong. I tried to teach him, but he wouldn't, or couldn't, hear me.

I cannot say I enjoyed feeling superior to him. After all, he was no different from 99.99 percent of blackjack players in the world, who hold all sorts of dubious theories about the game. But was there a part of me that was internally gloating? He was a gambler, I was a player—in effect, an investor, an asset manager. I knew more than he did about playing cards. I don't think I can absolutely deny feeling some primitive sense of competition. And was he proud of my career turn? My hunch is yes. Maybe my career confirmed some conception he held of being a young man, of the allure of the casino and the music of riffling chips on the green felt tables. His closest associate at the time was the younger brother of my principal backer, Johnny Francesco, so I assume he had plenty of inside information on the operation. One thing for sure was that my life as a counter playing blackjack around the world was something he could intuitively understand much better than my life as a teacher or poet or grad student. For a while, I could say the same about myself. As for his depths of understanding or empathy or curiosity, they were either nonexistent or inexpressible for the man called Popey. And he might have been fascinated by how I was playing with Other People's Money, and not money I borrowed or stole, but money entrusted to me. And when I played with OPM (technically, a small share of it was mine) and I won, I got to claim some of it as my own (well, my percentage of it anyway).

In the end, playing cards for money and gambling in general maybe wasn't in my DNA. Except for the times when I took my father to the track in his waning years and kept him company and bet alongside him, I haven't made a wager in thirty years, but I still pick the games for pure intellectual sport, the way other guys read the *Racing Form* every day, for pleasure. Take it from me: don't bet the favorite, automatically going in on what appears to be the more talented team. The better teams can and do indeed lose, and teams are more evenly matched than records and statistics superficially show. Sometimes the favorite convinces itself that it's the disrespected dog, and that's different, so they play hungry, but it's a subtle distinction hard to explain in the abstract. Underdogs almost always have more reason to play and to win, or at least to cover the spread, and that's why getting the points is valuable. Not that that is reason in itself to bet. Because don't forget rule number two: only losers robotically jump on a good team getting points, banking on covering. That's fool's gold. If you don't really believe the dog can win the game outright, it's usually prudent keeping your powder dry.

∾

IT'S ONE THING TO understand a capo of the crime families, the John Gottis, the Sam Giancanas of the underworld, or the monsters who became murderers and are bizarrely, cinematically lionized. It's another to understand the little guys who are doing all they can to scrape by. Hard to romanticize the kind of life my father led. And he was nowhere near a big fish. If he was offered Witness Protection and a new identity, I never heard about it.

All the same, my father rubbed shoulders with some very infamous figures in New York crime annals, such as the very big-time Columbo Family underboss Sonny Franzese, who lived in our neighborhood. And he seemed to cross paths with a made guy named Sebastian "Buster" Aloi, who is credited with recruiting Franzese into the mob and who was arrested twelve times during the course of his criminal career on charges ranging from gambling to murder. My father told me he worked as a bartender in a local joint. I speculate that the bar was operated if not effectively owned by Aloi, and that my dad did business with dirty cops who worked for or with Aloi. He could hardly be in the dark about the goings on of bookmakers, fixers, number runners, robbers, stick-up artists, shakedown specialists, loan sharks, burglary rings, and truck and air cargo hijacking crews operating in the neighborhood.

Along the way he also became acquainted with Mickey "Cheesebox" Callahan. Callahan enjoyed a reputation as being bookmakers' as well as corrupt cops' best friend. He was the notorious and preeminent "wireman" and the inventor of a device, the size of a pack of cigarettes, that could transfer phone calls so that bookmakers were able to take bets away from where the phone was situated. He would be the subject of a 1971 *New York Times* piece by the eminent journalist David Burnham (who broke the Serpico and Karen Silkwood stories), about Callahan the "inventor" going straight later in life. Before that career transformation, though, he was also expert at sabotaging official radio transmission of race results, so as to enable gamblers (like Al Capone, for whom he once worked) to past-post bets and clean up with bookmakers. (Al Capone!) He crossed the wrong guy, however, a mob associate of Aloi, who one night attempted to rub him out, only to shoot Callahan's son instead.

Sidney Cooper, with whom my father cooperated, was a captain in the Police Commissioner's Confidential Investigations Unit. One night in April 1961, when he arrested Callahan, he crowed that he had heard a lot about the famous Cheesebox but never thought he'd get to bust him.

"The pleasure is all yours," said Callahan.

Cooper told Callahan that he wasn't his real target, it was crooked cops. He tried to recruit him to work with the PCCIU.

"Captain, if you knew anything about me, you know I'd never be partners with cops. That's like taking a bath with alligators."

That was apparently not a sentiment shared by my father, or maybe that is a sentiment he could not afford to share. At one point he testified against a cop who was a neighborhood friend of his, Vincent "Jimmy" Santa, another associate of Callahan, who was known as the bagman of the Brooklyn Morals Squad. After Santa was drummed out of the police force, he reportedly became a full-fledged mobster, later convicted of truck hijacking, and did hard time. I always knew my old man was not exactly risk-averse, but I didn't know the depths of his recklessness and desperation.

As for his career paths, he did leave behind stonecutting. Silicosis is a very common affliction of a stonecutter. Silica is associated with lung cancer, and breathing it in over the long haul can lead to chronic obstructive pulmonary disease, especially back when my father was cutting stone and fewer state-mandated labor precautions were in place. The dust buildup in the lungs can accumulate and set like concrete. That's the sometimes deadly cost of making tombstones for strangers. My father's whole life, he seemed to be rolling the dice, always trying to suck in enough oxygen to breathe.

New York State Appellate Division

RECORDS AND BRIEFS

*I**f Your Honor please, I don't want to put you in the position of committing reversible error, there is a court of appeals decision, which I will bring to you before the next return date, which states I have the right to ask the witness as to any criminal activity which he has conducted...*

Now, this man is now apparently under arrest. Not out on bail, not in jail, he is being treated like a pet, he is being kept in a hotel because he can testify against cops. I intend to show that this is the motive to relieve himself of any punishment on the forgery charge he is presently facing, which prompts him to testify against these Respondents. You refuse to direct him to answer that question, puts me in the position of not being able to press this issue...

If Your Honor please, the reason the indictment is not being pressed [against Di Prisco] is because I intend to prove he received a promise to testify against cops, that's why the indictment is being held over his head.

Joseph DiPrisco, for Department, Cross

Q. Are you protecting them? A. I'm not protecting nobody.

Q. All right. Well, now you told us some story about a truck, this morning, do you remember that story? A. Yes, sir.

Q. When did that take place? A. In March.

Q. In March? A. The latter part of March.

Q. What was the name of the bookmaker? A. Cock-eyed Jerry.

Q. Cock-eyed Jerry. And you said somebody said they made a score, is that right? A. I was told a score was made.

Q. You were told that a score was made, is that right? A. Yes, sir.

Q. Now, did Mr. Celentano ever give you—did he—did he ever give you any money in connection with that supposed score, did he, yes or no? A. No.

Q. All right. Now, what was the next score? Was he present when anybody gave you any money? A. No.

Q. All right, now what was the next case, when you mentioned a score was made? A. Babe Dareda.

Q. Babe who? A. Babe Dareda.

Q. Did Mr. Celentano give you any money in connection with that supposed score? A. No, sir.

Q. Was he present when anybody gave you any money in connection with that supposed score? A. No, sir.

Q. Now, you said this morning, in connection with this truck deal, that somebody came back and said, "We scored." Is that right? Did I hear you right? A. That's right.

Q. They came back and said, "We scored.", is that right? A. Yes, sir.

Q. Well, that means they collected money, doesn't it? A. I mean they scored the bookmaker. They didn't arrest him.

TURF

Probably you've heard this one: there's one thing an Italian with dementia will never, ever forget—and that's a grudge. The folk wisdom might be confirmed by the science, and by my own personal experience: I am incapable of forgetting a real or perceived slight. Like father, like son?

Brain researchers say that long-term memory is the last to be vitiated by Alzheimer's; it's the short-term that is friable. And my dad did hang onto his grievances and grudges like they were family heirlooms. Which they were, in a way, because he persistently claimed to have been betrayed by his own family, his two brothers and one sister, who, in his view, ripped off his legitimate inheritance.

I overheard this accusation from early on, but was never presented the bill of particulars, so I never quite understood what his brief was against them. He was wronged, plain and simple. I knew it was disloyal of me, but I remained skeptical. And when his brothers or sister called on the phone, as they rarely did, my mother said he was walking the dog or something, even if he was sitting in front of the TV and even if we didn't then have a dog. If I had to hazard a hunch, I'd say his family might have been burned by him in the past. Maybe he borrowed money from them he never paid back, which he didn't pay back because he was entitled—he thought it was his birthright. Of course, the chance remains they refused to give him money he was entitled to because they were, in my mom's phrasing, "Italian fucking barbarians." Coin flip, I would say. It requires being a moron to bet on the outcome of a coin flip.

Over the years, and over the course of his accelerating dementia, my father was unsurprisingly consistent in his remarks about his past. So when I asked him periodically about the reasons for the flight from Brooklyn to California, he maintained that he was in trouble in New York City because he "had a lot of information" about cops, and that he was being "protected" in exchange for his testimony. He was being "squeezed," his term, by the FBI and the police. I asked him what he did to acquire that valuable information. He was evasive. No new development. He swam like a shark in a sea of evasiveness.

It becomes clearer in these NYPD hearings, and in the contemporary newspaper accounts, what he was up to. As a young man, he was habitually broke and an incorrigible gambler, and he relentlessly, intrepidly hunted for the cash to put down on the horses and then, when he lost, the cash to pay back the loan sharks and the others from whom he had borrowed it. Yet once, in a vulnerable-seeming moment, he acknowledged to me that he asked a made guy in the neighborhood for a loan, but was turned down. Why? The made guy said he wouldn't lend him the money because he liked him. The tale was spun as a point of pride.

At one stage, it seems, he was in the hole three thousand bucks, in debt for at least half of that to loan sharks, whom he and everybody else called "shylocks." Adjusting for inflation, that's about twenty-five thousand in today's dollars. Serious money, especially when you factor in loan sharks' draconian lending rates, which could escalate to 50 or 100 percent—a week.

He was also borrowing from at least three cops, and to pay them back he would engage in conspiracies to shake down bookmakers and parole violators. He would finger somebody, set them up, and then the cops would score them; that is, they would fake-arrest the mark, but would offer to make the arrest go away if they paid them off. Stakes were not trivial. In one instance, they shook down a couple of bookies for three thousand, quite a haul in the day. They paid my father $250 for his efforts.

～

HERE'S WHERE THE STORY gets a little more convoluted, if not deviously clever.

When I asked him what he did for the bookmaker he worked for, he would be less than clear. He wasn't one of those guys in green visors taking bets on the phone, spouting off the odds in a cloud of cigarette smoke, he explained. Though he sometimes did that on Saturdays, as he defended himself in court. That's when wiseass counsel reminded him that it was also illegal on a Saturday. And he also wasn't delivering bags of cash on square-up days to the rare-as-white-elephant winners, or threatening to break the legs of those who didn't or couldn't square up. "Tough guys collect," he said, implying he didn't qualify.

What he admitted to me was this: he was subverting the competition. That is, he took care of rival bookmakers who were, in his words, "stepping on our turf." This sounds like Brooklyn bookmakers' generally accepted best business practice.

A man named Joe Loguerico testified that he played a crucial supporting role in the Sal Valenti shakedown. He had known my father "at least twenty years" from the "old neighborhood, Greenpoint section."

> Q. *Did there come a time when you had a conversation with Joe Di Prisco regarding Sal the bookmaker?*
>
> A. *Yes.*
>
> Q. *What was the conversation?*
>
> A. *He wanted to know who I was betting with and I told him and he said he'd like to have him arrested. I went along with it and I told him I'd come walking out the building with him the following night.*

Q. *Was it mentioned by Di Prisco that you were to be paid for this?*

A. *He said he'd take care of me.*

~

So my dad would like to have a rival book arrested?

The conclusion we might draw from Loguerico's own words as well as my father's statement that he had a job dealing with guys who stepped on his turf is this: he seems to have been using the cops to eliminate or at least curtail the competition. The cops collected the shakedown money from the guys who didn't want, or couldn't tolerate, the bust, perhaps because they were on parole. Then, they seem to have shared some of the profits with him. Therefore, as the cops were using him as a confidential informant ostensibly in the service of the public good, they were in truth doing business for themselves. That also means that, as they were exploiting him, he was playing *them* to do the dirty job on the competition. It's easy to imagine—in fact, it's hard not to imagine—he was also making some money on the side from the bookmaker who employed him. Nothing of his working both ends of the deal ever came out in his testimony during cross-examination.

New York State Appellate Division

RECORDS AND BRIEFS

Q. And did you ever give him any information upon which he made any arrests?

A. Yes, sir.

Q. How many?

A. Quite a number of arrests.

Q. Information that you gave him where he didn't score, but made an arrest, is that right?

A. Yes.

Q. I mean, you didn't go into this stool pigeon business in order to be a shakedown artist, did you?

A. No, I just gave him the names of bookmakers, and how they worked.

Q. What is that?

A. I only gave names of bookmakers and how they worked.

Q. Yes, but you didn't do this because you wanted to help the police shake them down, did you?

A. I didn't do no shaking down.

Q. You wanted to help them find these gamblers, who you were betting with, is that right?

A. I just gave them names of bookmakers, how they worked, and they paid me for it.

Q. They paid you. You were making a couple of bucks on the side, is that right?

A. Yes, sir.

Q. Legitimately, is that right?

A. Yes, sir.

Pope and son; commencement.

Sealed Files

What did come out in the court records was that he had been extradited from California to New York City, and his rap sheet indicated pending charges in two jurisdictions, Queens and Brooklyn—numerous felony counts of forgery, burglary, and conspiracy. So where were his files, the record of the disposition of these charges? We found out six months after I delved into those trial transcripts on Google, around June 2015. The Brooklyn file seemed for now to be lost in limbo, but his case file in Queens, by an incredible stroke of luck, had survived a warehouse fire, where about half of the case files had been destroyed, but fortunately not his. When my industrious researcher, a former New York newspaper reporter, showed up in Queens, the court clerk said he did indeed have the file in his hand, but county counsel determined that the case file was sealed and therefore undisclosable to the public. How could that be? Why was the file sealed in the first place? I was determined to find out.

First, let's take two steps to the side.

THE FAST EDDIE F. COMPLEX

It was Sigmund Freud who once said, possibly after putting down his vial of cocaine and symbolic cigar for a minute, artists make art, and writers write, for the love of beautiful women. Let's have a look into Herr Doktor. His "science" has been systematically proven dead wrong about the unconscious, dead wrong about the Oedipus complex, dead wrong about penis envy, dead wrong about homosexuality, oh, the list goes on and on in an instance of his repetition complex, about which he was also dead wrong. His batting average is far below the Mendoza line, alongside some political eminences. Writing for the love of beautiful women, huh? That's the objective? And let's leave aside for a moment the reductive sexual assumptions implicit in his position.

Moment's up. Guy's a dog. By any measure and study, his very conception of psychoanalysis is bogus if not a failed treatment protocol. As a fabulist and mythologizer, however, Freud was a skillful and historically influential writer, so maybe if he wasn't hearing the

Siren's spoon call, he might have realized he was talking out of his bowler hat.

The motivations of writers may not always be of the virtuous variety, and they may be mystifying to writers themselves, and writers can be disreputable schemers and scammers, so give Freud very partial credit. But here's the small point I would make: writing is so hard that if a beautiful woman or man came up after a reading and said, "I love you, take me, I'm yours, you've changed my life, this is my cell phone number," I'm going to go out on a limb and say, "Is that all there is?" Of course, yes, indeed, true, sometimes it is all there is, but since when has it been enough? Hasn't everybody binge-watched *Real Housewives of The New York Review of Books*? Then again, I could very well be a disreputable schemer and scammer, and here's proof one way or the other: I wrote this book.

Full disclosure, or full enough: the psychodynamic model has its legitimate place, of course. It certainly had its place in my life, and the psychoanalytically inclined pediatrician and writer Winnicott is a genius I hold in the highest regard. And speaking of therapy, writing *Subway* was exhausting, like doing therapy on myself. At the end of each working day when the pace intensified over months and months, I was absolutely drained. Sometimes I wanted to send myself a bill.

And I resolved I would never write another memoir as long as I lived, it was too hard.

Yet here I am. Never trust a writer. But nobody needs to be reminded of that.

～

BEFORE PUBLICATION, I SHOWED my college girlfriend a draft of *Subway to California*, which contained more than a few pages about her and our mutual first-love relationship—now decades in the rear view mirror. I did not use her name, but I did identify her by her first initial. I thought my treatment of her was definitively on this side of reverential, and I stand by that general characterization to this day and always will. If anybody takes a hit in the book for what went wrong between us, it was me.

Post-college we remained friends, dear steadfast friends, after the requisite cooling off period, and we talked from time to time or visited with each other in California or New York. I had genuine regard for her brilliant, attractive children and husband, and she was on good terms with my wife and family. But in the pages I drafted I had done a bad thing. There was one sentence pertaining to her that she insisted I remove; though, as I said, her identity was completely concealed for the general public. In that sentence I incorporated an observation about—you know, it doesn't really matter what its essence or claim was. And no, no compromising or potentially embarrassing whips and bonds stuff, nothing remotely criminal or morally actionable.

The sentence wasn't critical to the narrative drift, and in context of the whole book it virtually amounted to a throwaway recollection, so I cut it. Still, it was no throwaway as far as she was concerned, it was hurtful to her and she was upset. Reluctantly, I could take her point. Had I completely misremembered or misread something about her? At first I was defensive and argued with myself that she was wrong and I was right, much the way I often did when we were involved. But what if I wasn't right? And if I wasn't, what else had I gotten wrong? I might have been a fool or an idiot or simply a wretched human being.

The iconic Russell Baker invoked a principle that has served as encouragement and instruction for any erstwhile memoir writer. He said nobody's life makes any sense, so tell a good story. Some cynical editors—cynical or wise, and excellent editors walk that high wire between those poles—have been known to say don't let the facts get in the way of telling the story. But when you write a memoir, your job is supposed to be different. It's the pact you have with your reader, whom you should never betray, ever. You are to tell the truth to the extent that you know it, if you aren't James Frey, that is, and I never read, and will never read, his book, not that there's any reason to pile on now.

A couple of years passed after she had read the draft. When I had come through New York in the past, I had normally made it a point to let her know and to get together, but I traveled there several times without contacting her, seeing no opening, and feeling sometimes annoyed, sometimes hurt, sometimes culpable. I am uncertain as to why or how a thaw took place between us. I am sure it took place on the occasion of a birthday phone call she initiated.

During that conversation she asked me if I was going to send her a copy of *Subway*, now in print. I was taken aback. "I think the last thing you said about the book was that you wanted nothing to do with it." She didn't deny she had said that. I couldn't resist asking if she realized books were a business, and they were available wherever fine books were sold—and yes, this was snarky of me, but she graciously ignored that. I told her I had not used her name or her first initial. "What did you call me?" She approved the choice of the name I used. I thought it was a great name, too. I pressed on. Why did she want the book from me now?

"Because I'm in it."

She was right, objection sustained. I sent her the book.

So when I heard about the sealed case files on my father, the one in Queens as well as possibly another one in Brooklyn, and I already had in my possession the trial transcripts that had recently appeared, I took a chance and gave her a call to give an update. She specializes in defending white-collar crime cases in New York City and was once a federal prosecutor, and I figured she would be expertly positioned, both professionally and personally, to do something about unsealing the file.

"This is getting seriously interesting," she said.

"Is it possible to unseal a case file?"

"Yes." But she was careful to qualify: possible didn't mean easy.

"I love you," I blurted out, surprising myself. It was at that moment that I realized all over again how I was all in on this investigation, how important the case was to me, and how important she was, too.

She laughed. "You haven't said that for a while."

Thus it was that Naomi took the case, not that that is her name.

Mitzvah Madness

O n another stop of the *Subway* tour, I did a reading at the Half King in Chelsea. This is a superb Irish literary bar with a very welcoming room for reading and a very desirable venue for authors.

Old college pals as well as friends from California and former students showed up, a nice little turnout. As I prepared myself to go on, dealing with pregame jitters and sipping on a shot of Irish to steel my nerves, a woman rose up from her table and walked over.

"Hi, I'm Patricia."

No clue. My brain scanned and scanned and scanned and spit out nothing. She cut me a break.

"I'm your cousin."

It clicked. Yes, she was. I saw it now. A first cousin I quickly calculated I hadn't laid eyes on for many decades, a daughter of my Uncle Mike and Aunt Ruth. Ruth was Jewish and therefore made for certain ridiculous complications for my ethnocentric Italian American family, but I liked her a lot. She was warm and kind and sweet to me when I was a little boy, and her three daughters were wonderful childhood playmates I thought I would never forget. But as tonight demonstrated, on that point I seem to have been overconfident.

My cousin and her husband, as it happened, lived on the road where my grandparents once had their farm and which was the launching point for my dad's self-appointed exile, and she had read the book. I had heard from her sister Jen that there was one aspect in particular that they appreciated. The memoir flickeringly brought to life on the page their loving mom, who had died when they were very young, so young in fact that they had precious little memory of her. This knocked me out.

I had made my share of questionable choices in the book, and obviously in my life for that matter, but this was one thing I had gotten a little bit right, even if I didn't know it, or intend it. Whatever gift I gave her, she had granted me something more precious.

Whose book was this again?

Consideration

In October 1961 the Police Commission called a single witness to testify against a decorated police sergeant, one Baldasaro "Benny" Ficalora. He, along with his partner, stood accused of shaking down a bookmaker named Sal Valenti, in 1957, for $600, which amounts to about $5,000 in today's dollars. Until my father appeared in New York City in September 1961, the police had no clue as to the Valenti shakedown. That meant he had been sitting on this information for use on a rainy day (such as being indicted, as he was). Either that or he had made up the story to get some play from the oncoming DA.

The transcript makes for fascinating reading, if by fascinating one means excruciating, forehead-smacking frustration. Under questioning, my father seems often confused, or feigns being confused—states of mind not readily distinguishable relative to him. Sometimes he's reticent, more than occasionally defensive. His thinking seems tortured, but *thinking* doesn't seem the word. His memory, overtaxed. His word choices, pokes in the eye with a sharp stick. He seems incapable of comprehending, much less responding to, direct questions. Or he understood them perfectly and didn't wish to answer. Then again, in my experience, he was always that way. Downtown Joe Di Prisco.

For example, under suppressive cross-examination fire pertaining to these dirty cops, he testifies that "they grabbed him," "him" referring to the bookmaker, Valenti. Counsel for the defense wanted to know, reasonably enough, who was "they."

"Tartarian [Ficalora's partner] got out of the car."

"It was not 'they,' just one man?"

"I got out, fingered the bookmaker to Tartarian."

"I'm asking you who is the 'they'?"

Counsel for the Department: "He said…"

Counsel for the Accused: "He didn't say."

For the Department: "He said it was Tartarian."

For the Accused: "'They' is not Tartarian."

For the Department: "To you it's not, to him it is."

For the Accused: "So is that what you mean, 'they' is one man?

"Tartarian got out of the car."

"You didn't mean 'they'?"

"Ficalora was at the wheel."

"You did not mean 'they'?"

"Well, only one man got out of the car. I can't say he didn't."

It goes on in this Runyonesque via Greenpoint fashion here and elsewhere for pages and pages—much like the unrecorded transcript of almost every conversation I ever had with him. His words are cumulatively reminiscent of nothing so much as a stoner version of Abbott and Costello's baseball vaudeville routine "Who's On First?" My father liked those comics.

> *Costello: Well then who's on first?*
>
> *Abbott: Yes.*
>
> *Costello: I mean the fellow's name.*
>
> *Abbott: Who.*
>
> *Costello: The guy on first.*
>
> *Abbott: Who.*
>
> *Costello: The first baseman.*
>
> *Abbott: Who.*
>
> *Costello: The guy playing...*
>
> *Abbott: Who is on first!*
>
> *Costello: I'm asking YOU who's on first.*
>
> *Abbott: That's the man's name.*
>
> *Costello: That's who's name?*
>
> *Abbott: Yes.*
>
> *Costello: Well go ahead and tell me.*
>
> *Abbott: That's it.*
>
> *Costello: That's who?*
>
> *Abbott: Yes.*

And no, English was not my dad's second language, though he makes it sound like he came through Ellis Island the week prior. More than anything, he seems to be heeding the stock wisdom of the streets: nobody was ever hanged for something he didn't say, something he couldn't deny, something nobody could understand. So he didn't express anything you could pin on him. This principle was absolute, and it applied not only to courtroom testimony, it also applied to the weather, to what he had for lunch, to how he was feeling today, to where he was going, to what he thought of the game, to what he wanted for Christmas. Plausible deniability was in his blood.

Of course, nobody should underestimate how stressful testifying under oath can be when counsel has painted a bull's-eye on somebody and is argumentatively skillful, able to distort a prepped witness's words. Equipped with his grade school education, my father distorted his own words enough for a courtroom of lawyers. What's more, for somebody like him, who I have no doubt in another era would have been diagnosed with attention deficit disorder, it had to be supremely challenging to think cogently and speak coherently at the same time—assuming cogency and coherence were his priorities, which it was not always clear they were. Compounding everything was that those felony charges were hanging over his head in the two boroughs over from Manhattan, where he sat in the witness chair. The prospect of execution truly concentrates the mind, as Samuel Johnson said, but in my father's circumstances, that seems a long shot. My general verdict on the old man's performance was not too bad, considering. He mostly held his own with the suits. *Not bad* was that Brooklyn man's highest accolade.

～

THE FORMAL CHARGES AGAINST Ficalora (and in other proceedings, his partner, Tartarian) alleged that he conspired with my father to frame the bookmaker Valenti in 1957. My dad used his old friend, Joe "Smokey" Loguerico, to help identify Valenti coming out of work, and then my father signaled in the police, who ushered Valenti into the backseat of Ficalora's car. That's when my father testified that he took an envelope from Valenti and said that there were numerous betting slips. At this point, it was contended, "having seized evidence of said crime [bookmaking], [Ficalora] did solicit, demand, and ask the said Valenti for a sum of money, in return for which the said Valenti would be released and freed from arrest." Valenti offered $200, but the cops said that wasn't enough. As my father predicted for Tartarian, Valenti would pay because he couldn't afford the pinch, or so Loguerico advised my father, and as a result he was summarily squeezed. My father took off at this point, and they drove the bookmaker to his home, where he came up with an additional $400, and that's where the matter lay dormant—until my father's extradition, when he testified.

In exchange for his information as confidential informant, my father received one hundred bucks from the cops, about eight hundred in today's dollars. He gave either twenty-five or fifty dollars to Loguerico, or so he said at various times, though Loguerico swore he never got a dime.

It would be easy to be suspicious of my father's testimony. After all, until he came back to New York, nobody knew the first thing about this shakedown. Seemed a little bit too convenient for somebody in tight straits like his. While counsel for the defense strained to establish that my dad made up the accusations out of whole cloth to save his own skin, giving something of value to the police so as to increase the chances that his own problems would go away, the two cops made some crucial errors that cast grave doubt upon their defense. For one thing, Tartarian denied using my father as a confidential informant as a regular practice, but that seemed not to be true upon examination. In fact, he had used him for years. "Tartarian was plainly inconsistent and evasive about his relationship with Di Prisco," ruled the Police Commission.

For another thing, Ficalora asserted that the car my father identified as being the one driven during the night of the shakedown could not have been his car, which, if so, should discredit Di Prisco's testimony and exonerate him. The 1949 Chevy, he said, had been junked before the night of the alleged crime. But police furnished records and other evidence indicating that that car had been operable on the night in question and that, in fact, Ficalora had unfettered access to the vehicle.

Once the hearings concluded, the deputy police commissioner formally weighed in on my father's status and commented on his testimony:

"It is conceded that there are several inconsistencies in Di Prisco's testimony and that he was not truthful at a previous departmental trial where he said that he did not know other policemen, wherein in fact he did. It is also conceded that his character and background are unsavory and that his relationship with the District Attorney, while under indictment at the time of his trial, provided a ready motive for his testifying against these respondents."

As they claim in country songs, you gotta dance with the one that brung you. Despite my father's "unsavory character," "Additional support for the credibility of Di Prisco's testimony can reasonably be found in the testimony of the men charged, which on crucial questions is so inconsistent and evasive as to permit the inference that had they testified in a straightforward manner, their guilt would have been apparent."

In the end, Benny Ficalora was dismissed from the police force, but though my father testified on this matter to the grand jury, he and Tartarian were not indicted.

∾

ON MANY FRONTS THE city was cracking down on police corruption, and the press was gearing up for big sweeps and crackdowns. As *The New York Times* reported, on April 24, 1962, Peter Celentano, a plainclothes Vice cop, was found guilty of consorting with gamblers, clearly a reference to my dad, and dismissed from the force. "He also had been linked with a paid informer"—also my dad. I am pretty sure my father never perused the *Times*. No copy ever showed up in our apartment. Back when there were eight metropolitan papers, he was a *News* and *Mirror* guy—at least those were the papers he usually sent me out to buy at the candy store on a Sunday morning. I wonder if he would have felt relieved not to be named. *The New York Herald Tribune* did name names, in "Cop Fired for a 'Shakedown'" on April 24, 1962:

"Peter R. Celentano, 27, working with an ex-patrolman dropped from the force last year, used a police informant 'to put the shake' on bookies and policy operators [number runners] who could not stand being arrested, according to the testimony of the informant, Joseph Di Prisco.

"Di Prisco testified...that he along with Celentano and Vincent Santa entered a conspiracy in which Di Prisco would give them the names of gamblers going full blast...

"Di Prisco testified that in March, 1961, he fingered a bookie operating in a truck. This was in violation of the bookie's parole. The

bookie thereupon was shaken down for $1,000, with Di Prisco pocketing

$100 and the rest going to the two officers, according to his testimony.

"About the same time last year, Di Prisco, through the two officers,
'put the arm' on a paroled policy operator, who shelled out $2,000, of
which Di Prisco got $250, he said.

"However, Di Prisco testified, there were times when in acting as
finger man for the two officers, they did their duty and made arrests,
shunning shakedowns."

That's interesting, and a curious turn. Wonder if it was true. But
if they didn't extract a payoff, the cops did my father a service by
popping his rivals.

RECORDS AND BRIEFS

While Di Prisco's identification of Respondent Ficalora was weak, this was explained by his admission that he did not know Ficalora too well, having only met him once and seen him a few times with Tartarian before the incident with Valenti. It is conceded that there were several inconsistencies in Di Prisco's testimony and that he was not truthful at a previous departmental trial when he said he did not know other policemen, whereas in fact he did. It is also conceded that his character and background are unsavory and that his relationship with the District Attorney, while under indictment at the time of this trial, provided a ready motive for his testifying against these Respondents.

Notwithstanding these facts, I am constrained by an analysis of all of the evidence to believe the essentials of Di Prisco's testimony which proves the charges against these Respondents...

There was nothing on the record to indicate that Valenti ever met Di Prisco between the time of the incident and the subsequent investigation by the District Attorney years later. It follows, therefore, that there was no opportunity for them to collaborate on a story. In *addition, the corroboration of the details of the incident by Valenti, a reluctant witness, and to a lesser extent by Lo Guericio, make it clear that Di Prisco's story is not a fabrication.*

Supreme Court—State of New York

Criminal Term—Part K-9 Queens County

~

THE PEOPLE OF THE STATE OF NEW YORK

-AGAINST-

JOSEPH DI PRISCO, DEFENDANT

IND. NO. 1120/1961

~

Not-Naomi, Esq., argued to unseal the Queens County criminal records. In the essential parts of her argument, she contended on behalf of the Movant, me:

```
Over half a century ago, on or about
September 28, 1961, Movant's father, Joseph
L. Di Prisco, was arrested in Queens County
```

on charges of forgery in the second degree and grand larceny. (A copy of Joseph L. Di Prisco's Criminal Record is annexed as Exhibit A.)

1. Unsealed contemporaneous records, available on Google, reveal that the case against Joseph L. Di Prisco was resolved in his favor. Presumably, the records pertaining to the case were then sealed in accordance with Criminal Procedure Law ("CPL") §160.50(1), which provides that "[u]pon the termination of a criminal action or proceeding against a person in favor of such person, … the record of such action or proceeding shall be sealed…". Notably, there are no other bases for sealing that could potentially apply here. Movant seeks all records and papers relating to his late father's arrest and prosecution in the criminal action identified herein.

2. Movant is entitled to the Sealed Records pursuant to CPL §160.50(1)(d), which provides that the records sealed under CPL §160.50(1) "shall be made available to the person accused or to such person's designated

agent…"

3. Joseph L. DiPrisco is dead. If he were alive, he would be entitled, as the accused, to unseal the records.

4. Movant should be authorized to unseal those records as his father's "designated agent" under CPL §160.50(1), as explained in his accompanying affidavit, sworn to on October 16, 2015 ("Di Prisco Aff."):

a. Movant was designated as his father's agent with broad powers when his father was alive, and was given a Durable Power of Attorney.

5. There is no countervailing justification to prevent access in this case. The Court of Appeals has explained that the legislative objective was remedial: to prevent a person charged but not convicted from suffering the by-products of an unsuccessful prosecution, such as unemployment or disqualification from a profession, licensing or job.

6. Here, the remedial legislative purpose underlying CPL §160.50 is not implicated because Movant's father is deceased. His arrest

took place over half a century ago.

7. Accordingly, pursuant to CPL §160.50, we respectfully request that the Sealed Records be released to Movant, as the son, heir and designated representative of the late Joseph L. Di Prisco, through his undersigned counsel and legal representative.

∾

THE DAY BEFORE THANKSGIVING, the judge rules in our favor.

The motion to unseal records is granted with appropriate redactions reflected on the copy provided to defendant's son.

This constitutes the decision and order of the court.

Date: November 25, 2015

∾

THE UNSEALED FILE CONTAINS various pieces of clarifying information as to chronology, the scope and scale of the crimes, and the role my father played in their commission. There is also a record of legal maneuvering: failure to appear; bench warrants issued and bail determined; arraignments; revocation of bench warrants, etc.

On December 11, 1962, he appeared before The Honorable J. Irwin Shapiro, roughly nineteen months after his initial flight from Brooklyn. I was twelve and I have no recollection of this trip to New York. I find it perplexing, if not unfathomable, that I can recall nothing pertaining to his extended periods of absence, nor anything about my parents' explanation, presuming they must have offered something, but it is indeed the case. If I had to take a wild guess, they probably intimated he had to leave town to work at another job. That sort of thing would have sounded credible enough for me not to register.

We know now that he had been indicted and arraigned in July 1961 and was arrested when (or possibly before) he appeared in New York, in September 1961, and that he had testified in assorted cases during that fall. Before Judge Shapiro, the People are represented in 1962 by Assistant DA Bernard M. Patten, who weighs in:

If Your Honor pleases, this defendant was indicted on an indictment charging forgery in the second degree–six counts, grand larceny second degree–four counts, attempted grand larceny second degree, and conspiracy, along with a codefendant, [NAME REDACTED]. The evidence against this defendant came about by way of the testimony of a coconspirator who was not indicted by the Grand Jury and was given immunity. Further, there were wiretaps introduced into evidence before the Grand Jury. [NAME REDACTED] made a motion to inspect the Grand Jury minutes, and as a result of that motion, on October the 3rd, 1961, Judge Bosch dismissed the indictment against [NAME REDACTED].

Now I have been in touch with this situation for the last few years and in my opinion [NAME REDACTED] is the main conspirator in

this case. Di Prisco in my opinion was a tool of [NAME REDACTED].
I'm confident that if Di Prisco himself had made a motion to inspect
the Grand Jury minutes, the same reasoning that Judge Bosch gave in
deciding the indictment against [NAME REDACTED] probably would
apply; but aside from that, there are some times I suppose when the
District Attorney has to consider the equities involved, and in my opinion
Di Prisco is not as culpable as [NAME REDACTED] and yet [NAME
REDACTED]'s not before this court, and yet after the indictment of this
man, I've gone into his background and I'm satisfied that he has been
rehabilitated. …but I tell you this, your Honor, that I believe that this
man is not at this time in a position to be a recidivist. His wife and
family live in California. He has the prospect of a good job.

Then in view of the "equities involved," he requested that Di
Prisco's indictment be dismissed. "There are other considerations,"
he further explained, which he is not willing to "spread on the
record." Doubtless, he was referring to my father's cooperation with
law enforcement in the prosecution of other crimes. The Court
acknowledged it had been apprised of the details off the record, and
in short ordered the indictment to be dismissed.

"Defendant is discharged," ruled Judge Shapiro.

∽

SCALE AND SCOPE OF the crimes? Not the JFK Lufthansa heist.

He was charged with six counts of forgery on checks to some individuals and two grocery stores between 9 and 13 February 1961, all in the same mysterious amount, $105.75, which would amount to a not-trivial haul at the time. Those crimes were deemed Forgery in the Second Degree, and four counts of Grand Larceny in the Second Degree, along with ancillary charges including conspiracy as a misdemeanor. He was indicted along with another man, [NAME REDACTED], who was given immunity, probably in order to secure cooperation in another criminal investigation. The man's identity was tantalizingly surmisable upon a review of the entire file and the transcripts; the coconspirator was no one other than the eminent Cheesebox Callahan, for whom my father was an uwitting pawn, according to the ADA. One key piece of evidence: the unsealed indictment details that my dad met [NAME REDACTED] at what was Callahan's Queens workshop-office address. For years, then, it seems my father travelled along in the same universe with the likes of Callahan and mobsters such as Santa and Aloi. Maybe my dad owed Callahan money, and maybe that explains the checks. He wasn't the first and he wasn't the last gambler or loan shark to whom he might have been indebted.

Even so, the file contains confirmation of the district attorney's willingness to go to bat for my father. In a memorandum dated January 25, 1962, re: PEOPLE AGAINST DEPRISCO [sic], ADA

Patten, Chief of Homicide & Investigations Bureau, gives the court assurances that Di Prisco will appear as promised, as soon as he returns from California. To that end, he requests an adjournment to accommodate his travel schedule. Kind of the gentleman.

Now, all that was left for him to deal with was the charges in Brooklyn. And his family in California.

One last thing: as for uncovering his criminal files in Brooklyn, we struck out. They had been destroyed in a warehouse fire.

CIAO, BELLA

They say learning a second language guards against cognitive decline.

From childhood I exclusively identified with my father's Italian heritage, and not my mother's Polish. I formally started learning Italian comparatively late, though as a child I could somehow communicate with my Italian immigrant grandparents, who spoke very minimal English. If the brain researchers know something, I might have a shot. Once a good friend and I were in a fabulous *enoteca* in the Tuscan countryside. Everybody calls him "Primo" after a character in that funny, sad, nostalgic movie *Big Night*, which is centered on two restaurateur brothers anticipating the arrival of the then-popular singer Louis Prima (whose presence would advance the restaurant's reputation, but who in the end, spoiler alert, never materializes); it is equally centered on the creation of a *timballo*, an incredibly elaborate and delicious pasta and pastry concoction that (trust me) you need to free up a couple of days in order to construct. Our enoteca owner had zero English, but we were emboldened and we jabbered self-assuredly. Then a fairly gorgeous, statuesque, blonde German woman sauntered in, overheard our nattering, and ventured in Italian with a crafty smile, "You guys speak pretty good Italian." We preened and tut-tutted, modestly full of ourselves. She proceeded to qualify precisely what she meant: that we spoke pretty good Italian "per Americani." *Sheisse, fräulein, auf wiedersehen.* Nowadays, after ten years of studying, in classes and with private tutors and by frequent travels and after matriculating at language schools in Italy and California, my Italian skills are receding by the day. I can feel the loss, to my mournful disappointment and sadness. There must be a suitable aria to sing from Puccini, because isn't there always? I hope the loss is temporary, fleeting. Once I had pretty good command of the two past tenses and the fucking ridiculous subjunctive (which they call the fucking *congiuntivo*, don't get me started). I rambled through books by Alberto Moravia and Italo Calvino and Natalia Ginzburg among other great writers in the original Italian. For fun, I powered through the Italian translations of *The Great Gatsby* and *Catcher in the Rye*, which might have constituted dirty pool on my part, because I knew every English sentence by heart already. As I studied, I could easily draw on idiomatic expressions from my brain's linguistic ATM. In class I could venture an R-rated joke in Italian my endearing Italian teacher chuckled over. (My teacher, who was amused and who herself had very little English, once memorably mentioned that she had recently done some excellent shopping in a store she called *Bed, Bath, and Behind,* which name I think should be adopted immediately.) My wife is off the scale when it comes to language. She can speak in many tongues, so she is very useful in airports (and everywhere else), and her French is absolutely perfect (so I have heard a hundred native speakers tell her). Her Italian accent isn't quite as good as mine, but she can communicate effortlessly in Italian. Only now my Italian is like an overconfident swimmer who has swum out too far from the Mediterranean shore, swept gently along by the caressing tide. I'm hoping the currents will turn and bring it back to me someday. That would be a lifesaver.

They say learning a second language guards against cognitive decline.

⤿

MOVIE CLICHÉS OF THE Italian home: big, bombastic, boisterous feelings, usually of rage and injured merit. Platters of pasta and sausage. Reeking garlic sautéed in the pan. This was my grandparents' home, but it was not my Greenpoint home. My mother didn't really cook Italian, and she would sooner eat glass than garlic. My Polish mother's stock take on the whole Italian *thing*: "They're all fucking barbarians, these Italians." I didn't care what she thought, I mean I did care because she was my mother, but I wanted to be a barbarian like that.

⌒

SOME FRIENDS OF MINE got married in Rome on a beautiful June night. He is Italian, she is Canadian, they met in Paris, and theirs was a lovely wedding and a great celebration at a museum. In case you ever wondered about an Italian wedding party, rest assured that no Judd Apatow or Adam Sandler movie bromance ever threatens to break out. The food and wine are better than the typical catered American event. People dress better, too, all of the guests looking effortlessly, almost thoughtlessly stylish. But hand an Italian guy a mic at the reception and, surprise, he doesn't croon like Dean Martin or Andrea Bocelli. Because Italian wedding toasts are pretty much on par with the toasts at your second cousin's postprandial roasting in Philadelphia or Seattle—remember high school, remember his old girlfriend, remember when she threw onto the street his T-shirt collection…

At this wedding, there was one remarkable development. During those endless, repetitive toasts, a news flash shuddered through the assemblage like mainlined gelato headache. Two guests, a man and a woman, had been come upon in the women's bathroom and, umm, interrupted, right there in the act, *in flagrante*. Both of them married, too. That's not the unprecedented part. There are a lot of

Italian movies with a scene similar to that—could be tragic, could be comic, you never know for a while in an Italian movie. Yet here at this wedding the Italians were horrified. Also not unusual: their theatricalized horror. Italians do high dudgeon with the best Turkish rug traders, who are fake-insulted by your daring to bargain.

No, the Italian wedding guests were horrified, not because these two wedding guests were cheating, randy married people, but because they were married to each other. The act was conjugal. What, had they no connubial dignity? Did somebody lose a bet? Why didn't somebody think of the children!

The band was cued, and the night went on. And on. Like in Philly or Seattle. With better food and wine.

∽

PROBABLY OBVIOUS, SO APOLOGIES, but to review, in case:

Ciao, bella: used familiarly to address a female.

Ciao, bello: used familiarly to address a male.

In other contexts, where you might risk sideways glances after presumptuously saying *ciao* to the wrong person, you cannot go wrong saying *Salve* (hi or bye) or *ArrivederLa*. But you save the *Arrivederci*, or the sweeter *Ci vediamo dopo* (we'll see each other later), for more familiar contexts.

It might indicate something profound, or at least comforting, that *ciao* means both hi and bye. Something about the fluidity and mutability of time and social circumstance, which the Italians know all too much about. Or maybe it's simpler: it's such a universal, perfectly supple mouth- and ear-pleasing word.

～

ITALIANS LOVE THEIR AUTOMOBILES; Fiats seem to outnumber pedestrians on the thoroughfares of Rome, where I was once struck by one—another story. During the World Cup every Italian is certifiably *pazzo* for soccer, but racecar driving is right up there, too, in the fanatical national consciousness. Ferrari and Lamborghini and Bugatti and Maserati and Alfa Romeo—these are iconic, stunning, jaw-dropping vehicles and hundred-mile-per-hour works of art.

For as long as I can remember, I yearned for an Italian car of my own. It's awkward to own up to such an adolescent fantasy, but there it is, and it isn't my sole adolescent fantasy, as was transparent to my exes if not yet to you. In any case, much later in life, I realized I might be able to make this fantasy come to life.

Now, the hedonic research indicates that happiness proceeds not so much from possessing things as from enjoying experiences. I got that. But driving a certain kind of Italian car would be an experience disguised as a thing. So perhaps one day I could get lucky, could swing a deal for a used one. And it would be all-right-just-give-me-my-speeding-ticket-already flame red. Ideally it would not merely be fast, but gorgeous.

According to his estate, my father had bequeathed me his newish upscale Japanese car and some cash. (Long before he passed, I had seized the keys and his driver's license, and parked the car at my home, where he couldn't gain access to it; his doc determined that in his impaired state he was a danger to himself and others behind the wheel.) His Lexus was a very sound car, and practically in mint condition, except for the series of door dings and scratches accumulated in his bumper-car senescence. Unexpectedly, I had to process complicated emotions. I didn't want to keep his car; it wasn't my kind of car. No disrespect, as New Yorkers offer before being disrespectful. But was I being disloyal to his automotive memory? And to my mother's? The personalized license plate did read *CAZA*, which was her nickname, short for Cashmera.

I wasn't sure, but two years after he died I decided to go for it. Parlaying the trade-in with the inherited small cash windfall, I had enough to buy an Italian beauty, and it was fast, too. Onlookers thought it was a babe magnet, and it sort of was, but it was maybe more of a teenage boy magnet.

Fathers and sons, men and boys, and their cars: this whole book might be a footnote in a study of the subject.

I took possession of the dream about a month before a buddy's father passed. Billy's big Irish family counted as a kind of second home to me in high school, and I always liked his folks and his brothers and sisters. In fact, three of Billy's sisters sometimes babysat Mario when he was a little fellow, and all of us guys cultivated chaste crushes on these adorable colleens. The last time I had seen his now-deceased dad was at the funeral for his mom, a couple of years before. Bill Senior may have been in the advanced stages of dementia, but when I approached him to express my condolences, before I could get out more than a word or two, he said, with a wry smile and question mark, "Joe Di Prisco?" We shook hands and that was the entire, moving exchange. Billy couldn't believe his dad's memory had kicked in for a moment.

The family was holding an Irish wake in a Catholic church across town on a Friday night. Italians and the Irish, Irish and the Italians: both susceptible to ethnic stereotypes. Irish invented talking, Italians invented never shutting the fuck up. Poets and brawlers, both. Both cops and mobsters, sometimes simultaneously. Stereotypes may come in handy, as each contains a germ of truth. Therefore it takes a fool to subscribe. Italians and Irish. They are exactly the same, only completely different. Though only one has a cuisine. But I wouldn't dare say as much in that gathering.

It was a dark and stormy February 6. This meant a memorable anniversary for me: the date on which my beloved brother Eddie died in 2002 in New York City, and also the date on which my beloved dog, also named Eddie and also now dead, was whelped in 1998. The most direct route to the services for me was over the hills, Wildcat

Canyon Road through Tilden, the beautiful regional park. It might be unwise driving in such tempestuous weather, but the car had such fabulous traction, perfect for blustery conditions, and I could not resist. I could also rationalize it needed to be run out—there were few miles on the odometer.

Once on my way, true to form, the car was handling like a thoroughbred, with assurance and command on the twisty two-lane roads devoid of all other traffic. Huge winds were gusting and rain was pouring down, *a catinelle*, as the Italians idiomatically put it, in buckets. It may have been crazy, driving up here in a gale, but it was exhilarating as a roller coaster ride.

I made the wide turn, coming around a blind, as I approached Inspiration Point, and...

Have you ever watched a hundred-foot-tall pine tree crashing down in your direction? Me, either, till that night. It was a surreal vision. I slammed the world-class brakes and came to a stop a mere couple of feet in front of the tree. Funny thing about the flood of adrenaline—it doesn't jack you up, it slows everything down, and you become preternaturally calm. It was the next day that reality slammed home and I sought out the Valium.

What if I had been driving five miles faster? No doubt about it: one second, maybe a half second, away from a formerly pristine and now scrap-heaped Italian car, and its crushed Italian American driver.

If things had turned out differently, I could imagine the eulogies delivered by my wiseass friends. Talk about luck of the Irish. What kind of mook gets permanently pancaked on the way to a funeral? Leave it up to a crazy Catholic, giving up the ghost on the way to honor the deceased. And after all his close calls and risky moves throughout his life, it was a tree that took out the guy. A fucking tree. What a sad, sad waste—of such a gorgeous car.

New York State Appellate Division

RECORDS AND BRIEFS

Q. That statement was untrue?

A. Actually it was untrue.

Q. And you were under oath, weren't you, you know what I'm getting at now?

A. I was under oath.

Q. You made a false statement under oath?

A. I did.

Q. Now, you remember Ficalora, don't you?

A. No, sir.

Q. You don't remember him very well?

A. Only met him—met him and seen him a few times.

Q. How many times did you see him?

A. I seen him in the presence of John Tartarian.

Q. When and where?

A. Just passing in the car when I—in Queens.

Q. You what?

A. Just passing in a car.

Q. And you winked?

A. No, I said I seen him passing in the car with Tartarian.

Pope jitterbugging in the Atlantic, WWII.

MORE ALIVE THAN EVER

I was late to the memoir party with *Subway to California*, but then again, the better parties always start late and then hold out the promise or threat never to stop. My poet friends blanched. "How's your Me Moir going?" they'd ask, nyuck nyuck elbow to the ribs, implying I should be doing something more worthwhile, like writing poems. As if poets weren't as self-involved as anybody, come on, as if. My novelist friends pitied me; I was pathetic, talking about myself, advertising myself and my precious little sensibilities. My female book-loving friends totally in jest wanted to know what possessed me to dare encroaching onto their territory.

My son weighed in indirectly, as is his style. Well, he did explicitly say two things. First, he didn't figure me for a chemical dependency. (That made two of us.) Second, for him, in the book I was kinder on the subject of his mother than he expected. But he is not always the forthcoming type, and he is extremely diplomatic, which is to be expected of the only child of an unstable couple such as his mom and I were. I am used to reading between his lines, and sometimes I get it right, and besides, I emotionally leak enough for any room full of people.

I also overheard, at my mother's funeral, an exchange between him and a cousin, when she asked him if he was *worried* his dad was writing a memoir. "Worried?" Mario said. "I don't know, but it seems like there are two kinds of memoirs. One where you land a plane on the Hudson. And the other, which involves hookers and blow in Las Vegas. As far as I know, my dad never landed a plane on the Hudson."

I dedicated the book to him anyway.

I TRAVELED DEEP INTO THE farthest hinterlands of Memoiristan, and I read around as I typically do, promiscuously, randomly, idiosyncratically. In my uninformed opinion, which I would defend to the death, there exists roughly about the same percentage of great memoirs as the percentage of great books period—that is, not high. There are obviously first-rate autobiographical reads out there: accounts of religious conversion, of drug and alcohol dependency, of combat, of teaching, of sex, of dying, of childhood trauma, of entrepreneurial vision, of leadership, of crime, of the life of a writer, of cultural crossing, of insane family, *family,* and more family still—lots of books about the family, which probably makes sense, given that our first conception of ourselves begins in that hurly-burly, knockdown drag-out melee called home. First *conception* of ourselves? Maybe I mean instead that's when we begin to mythologize ourselves, or resist the temptation to do so and tell the truth about the messy lives we actually led and lead. As a very devout little Catholic boy I had a beautiful stained-glass window onto the mythologization of my soul, my passage through this temporal vale of tears on the way to eternal life. Amen. To be candid, I still like that view, though the scenery has radically altered since childhood.

One objective of *Subway* was to gain a handle on the story of my father's life, not easy to do when Sphinxes are more forthcoming than the old man, and I know that sounds suspect if not bizarre given his apparent and strategic forthcomingness in court. It was not so long ago that I had less information then than I have now, and if I sometimes wonder what it would be like to present some of my findings to him, now that he's gone, I realize probably that wouldn't have gotten me too far. As a young boy I always wanted more of him, and never got it, though my mother always insisted I was "the apple of his eye," something I by and large missed during his lifetime.

Now that he's dead, my father seems more alive than ever; he seems immortal.

New York State Appellate Division

RECORDS AND BRIEFS

Q. Well, were you gambling at that time?

A. Yes, I was on unemployment.

Q. And were you using that money?

A. Well, sometimes I'd use it.

Q. Well, let me ask you this, did you make any loans with anybody?

A. Yes.

Q. And how much money was loaned to you?

A. Well, I owed about $1,500, "shylock" money.

Q. How much money would you say you were in debt for now?

A. About $3,000.

Q. And this money that you were in debt for, where did the money go?

A. Gambling.

Q. You mean playing the horses?

A. Yes, sir.

Q. Dice games, and the like?

A. Yes, sir.

Q. Did you ever discuss your personal financial problems with Celentano?

A. Yes, sir, he knew I was strapped, he knew I was in debt.

Q. How did he know you were strapped?

A. Well, I used to tell him I owed money to "shylocks," and things.

Q. Let me ask you this, prior to the scoring of Jerry, and Dereda, did you play with them?

A. Yes, sir.

Q. Lay bets with them?

A. Yes, sir.

Q. And after Dereda was scored, did you play with him?

A. Yes, sir.

Q. Well, why?

A. Well, this way they wouldn't be suspicious of anything.

Q. That you fingered them?

A. That's right.

BETWEEN HE AND I

The *Subway to California* published in 2014 was not the first book I wrote using that title. What I mean is, my book was in preproduction, had an ISBN number, and was scheduled for 2012. The manuscript was line-edited, the book jacket art was ready (featuring a grainy noirish photo of me in a Verona train station), the catalogue printed with the synopsis couched in that typically twee book-marketing prose that can often be tinctured beyond purple, more like eggplant: *melanzane*. Incidentally, although I have Italian blood flowing in my veins, I don't love eggplant—or capers, now that I think about it.

Jack Pendarvis wrote a fictitious "Spring Catalogue" in the service of imaginary books to be published by a fictitious company. Catalogue copy for *So Twines the Grape* goes like this: "Greeves-Dunn uses the tractor of her talent to plow the fallow Southern fields of genius, uncovering the cracked bones of truth and planting the seeds of a fiery enema for the soul." Hello, book clubs everywhere. Who wouldn't wish to buy that book, besides nobody? My synopsis sounded a little bit more promising, not that we field-tested it; you'll have to take my word for it.

Then my publishing house, and Pendarvis's, MacAdam/Cage of San Francisco, hit the skids. It had published my first three novels, enjoyed an extended and occasionally spectacular run as a darling of independent publishing, producing a few big bestsellers (not to be confused with my works) turned into major motion pictures. There is a sad and convoluted and instructive tale somebody should tell one day about MacAdam/Cage and the charismatic David Poindexter who founded and owned the house—but it won't be told by me. David had flaws, and some of them were doozies, and he cultivated his share of enemies, but nobody was smarter, or slicker, than he—and I guess I intend *slicker* to work at least two ways, one of them not being the good sort, and the other meaning dazzling. He was a legendary publisher who communicated passionate support of a writer, at least he did so for me, including when I sniffed the wafture of his bullshit in the air. Yes, writers can be the neediest of sorts. Sometimes a beautiful illusion will suffice. David could talk books without cease and was a fabulous drinking companion, funny, smart, generous, perhaps overgenerous. But all of a sudden—actually not so all of a sudden, which is why this is a story that might be told someday—he couldn't pay his bills, and after years of struggling the house was destined for Chapter 11. This was around the time he was diagnosed with terminal cancer, and it wasn't long before charming David died. His loss is a huge one for books, his friends and family, and for me personally. I miss him. Not that there weren't issues left unresolved at his death, but here is not the place to discuss them.

My first novel was one of the first few books published by MacAdam/Cage, and my third was one of the very last. The house was set to publish *Subway to California*, but that list of books never saw the light of day, and I am relieved, not that I felt that at the time, because at that juncture I was crestfallen. Here is why.

Some may call this madness, but I had composed ur-*Subway* half in first-person narrative and half in third-person narrative. You should read back that last sentence, because it may be unbelievable but it's true. That is, pages were printed in clearly demarcated, visually distinct sections: "I" and "me" in the italicized parts alternated with "Joe" and "he" and "him" in standard font. The book should have included a cigarette-pack-like black-death warning: "Reading blocks and blocks of italicized text may induce migraine upon the unsuspecting." You cannot imagine how difficult it proved to manage the pronoun antecedents, but that was just for openers. I somehow persuaded everybody—my agent, my editor, my publisher, all of whom had been initially skeptical.

I know. Brilliant, high-concept stuff, right? Writers have to spend too many hours arguing into their mirrors. I don't know if any memoir has ever been published using such a device, but there is at least one renowned memoir written in the third person, *The Education of Henry Adams*, a great book published in 1918, and it's an autobiography, but it's in the third person, which is the point I am belaboring. Sadly, his book is not much read these days, which others might be better positioned to explain. I have another story to tell, and the Adamses and Cabot Lodges and the Harvards in his memoir, while riveting and vividly rendered, had little in common with the Di Priscos and the Greenpoints in mine.

Here's how my ur-book came to be composed, if I may employ the passive voice. One day I wearied of the pestering *I*, all insistent upon *myself*, thinking it was all about *me*, which it was, but still. And then I performed an experiment. I started writing about *him*, who was of course *me*, and for reasons I cannot explain the sentences flowed and memory awakened, and pages generated themselves. It was as if by reducing the apparent level of self-consciousness in the prose styling, I could become freer to write my own story. I could almost believe I was being more objective and fearless. So far so good.

After MacAdam/Cage's sad demise, I had a new publisher. We were moving fast toward publication. My assigned editor was astute. He had edited two previous novels of mine, and knew his way around a manuscript. I largely trusted his judgment, gave in when I thought I should, stood my ground other times. For one thing, he was promoting a subtitle that I thought was his idea of a bad joke: "A Cautionary Tale to Live By." I said, Umm, get out, no way. The book was the hybrid third and first and my editor indicated that he was, well, onboard with that. But then he asked a question—I cannot recall the exact question, but I recall the tone. Never trust editors who don the velvet glove; they're hiding brass knuckles. The question was framed too gently for me not to be suspicious he was conveying a doubt, and more than that a misgiving that my book was trying too hard. He didn't use the word, but *gimmick* is what I heard.

That narrative scaffolding had enabled me to rig the draft, but so what? Did it serve anybody anymore? I slept on the possibility that it amounted to nothing but a cheap trick, this meritage blending of the third and the first, and stupidly show-offy, which was worse. By morning light I determined: either *he* and *him* or *I* and *me* had to go. I made my move. Over the next four weeks, I rewrote the entire book in the first person, and that's the way it would be published. I haven't heard a peep from *him* since and may *I* be forgiven for his sins.

Fresh Head

I couldn't estimate how much my dad squandered gambling, but I can hear my mother screaming at him over the decades about the thousands upon thousands of bucks he "pissed away." He never did buy a house, which didn't really trouble him, so I gather he never thought to sock away money for a down payment. He preferred to "invest" his funds elsewhere. He did ultimately lose the interest in betting the ponies when the Alzheimer's seized him, but that was not until he was well into his eighties. He was a good handicapper, however, which might sound funny given his track record. I wouldn't know from personal experience, but my guess is you would have to be a superhuman handicapper to stay in the black, much less make a living off playing the ponies.

He did declare bankruptcy once, in the late 1960s. This development sounded grim to my adolescent ears, and later I published a poem related to the subject that caught his eye, the one poem of mine he ever mentioned. He ran across it in my first book of poems, which was published with some small fanfare by a university press when I was twenty-five, a poem entitled "My Father Declares Bankruptcy," which ends this way:

I notice my name

Is missing from the list of creditors.

How much do I owe? What court can settle

Our accounts?

All right, it ain't "Ode to a Nightingale," and he made brutally clear he didn't like it, but unlike with Keats and his moronic critics, no great poet was devastated as a result. Others might share his low opinion, though maybe not the editors of the respected literary magazine that initially printed it. When I presented my parents a copy of the book I presumed neither of them would open it. My father's take on the whole poetry enterprise was blunt: "Won't pay the light bills," he declared. True enough, but who tipped him off? Beyond that, I felt terrible that I had hurt his feelings, not that that was my intention. I couldn't defend myself.

He often said to me, and he might have said as much that impromtu poetry review day, "You got some kinda fresh head." It might have been a common expression, but I cannot recall anybody else ever saying that. What did *fresh head* connote? It seemed to indicate something like naïve, or stupid, or overambitious, or overreaching, or foolish, or pathetic. All those meanings would have fit the context, given his dismissal of me.

He did not pursue a lifelong career as a small-time criminal. In fact, once he got to California, I have no solid information that he was ever again up to his old tricks—except for gambling. Instead, he worked in one dairy or another, in the freezer or driving milk trucks, mostly. He brought home lots of milk, butter, and ice cream, which we were made to understand was a perk of the job, and I have no suspicion he was stealing, but maybe I do indeed have a fresh head.

Whatever his vocational aspirations may have been as a young man, besides gambler, I have no idea. But his life did indeed take a remarkable turn in the 1980s.

✑

THAT WAS WHEN HE got involved in labor union politics, and won nine consecutive elections, first as a business agent and then as secretary-treasurer (effectively the chief operating officer) of a Teamster milk drivers' local in the East Bay. He took pride in the job and worked very hard, and gave every evidence of relishing the schmoozing and deal-making and breaking bread—as he liked to term it—that came with the job. His executive style filtered down into his home. When he left a note on the breakfast table, to get his wife's attention he wrote at the top, in big neatly shaped letters, "MEMO." And when his grandson got his first big job, he was suitably proud; once the boy became partner in the firm, the labor organizer saddled him with a new identity: Mario became "Management." This happened when my son, fresh out of college, chose to live with his grandparents for about a year in an arrangement they all relished.

Obviously, my father was well-liked—*nine* straight election victories don't happen by pure chance. Whatever he did to be effective in a charged political and business context, he must have possessed mad skills at compartmentalization. He negotiated complex union contracts, he fought off adversaries, he sat across from the fat cats who owned the companies and seemed to hold his own. He must have thought consecutively around people who weren't in his family. He must have taken notes, and when he gave speeches to the rank and file he must have made sense and been persuasive. His Brother Teamster leaders always spoke of him in laudatory terms. *Nine* consecutive elections is no small feat.

Recently I came across a flyer printed for one of his early reelection campaigns for business agent that went out to the rank and file, to invoke wonderful union lingo. If memory serves, and I'm certain in this case it does, I composed some of it, or at least revised it, relying upon his notes and a rough draft he handed over. If I couldn't be 100 percent certain, I would guess I did contribute because he couldn't type, and his prose wasn't consistent in terms of standard syntax or grammar. Unlike with my poetry, my prose composition efforts must have met with his approval. And I must have felt pretty good about it, too, because I kept a few flyers, which I came across some thirty or so years later at the bottom of a file drawer when I moved offices.

◁

DEAR SISTERS AND BROTHERS:

Some people learn on the job.

Some people learn from the job.

As your Business Agent these last three years, I did both.

There's nothing fancy about being a Business Agent. It just means working hard for you all day long. That's something you can't learn in schools or conferences. Every day—every single day since you voted for me—I have had the chance to serve my brothers and sisters in the Union.

[He details a few of his specific accomplishments.]

But this sounds like I'm blowing my own horn. And I know as well as anyone that there's always a lot more to do, always a long way to go. How many nights I spent at some plant working out a tense situation. How many times I cooled off an angry or an unreasonable employer. How many late night and early morning phone calls from my brothers and sisters who felt misused or wronged. As I say, there's a lot more to do.

I've been a member since 1962. I know the jobs and the plants from the inside. I've been a boxman and a cleanup man, I've worked in ice cream production, milk production, and as an ice cream truck driver.

I understand first hand the hard work you're doing. You can bet one thing: I won't forget any of that when I sit down at the bargaining table.

Let's talk. I want to let you know what I stand for.

I want to keep working for you. Everyday, as your Business Agent, I'm on your time.

᨞

ONE COULD HIGHLIGHT THE self-conscious disparagement of formal schooling, or underscore his righteous pursuit of justice on behalf of the put-upon working stiff. Equally, though, one could note the overriding sincerity of his tone, as well as his appeal to the fundamental fair-mindedness of his adopted brothers and sisters. He mixed in self-advertisement with modest self-abnegation. Nice touch, no? And he wanted them to appreciate in no uncertain terms that he understood firsthand the hard work they were paid to do, for which they should be paid more after he negotiated the next contract. He pleaded for their trust, which he hoped he had earned. And they gave it to him: they reelected him, again and again.

(Side note: having a sealed criminal file, as he did indeed have, would have been a boon to his employment or election prospects, because being a convicted felon would have conceivably jeopardized his union ambitions—the feds were all over the Teamsters, after all.)

He was also pragmatic and anything but sanguine as to the benefits of organized labor. For instance, when I was a restaurant general manager I detected the grouchy stirrings of a unionization effort led by a few malcontents. My dad gave me counsel off the record. (Now that I think about it, everything he ever said to me seemed to be off whatever the record could possibly be.) I may have asked for some advice; I cannot recall. And neither can I summon up the substance of his advice on how to avoid the complications of a union shop. I do recall that we made the facts abundantly clear to employees: our wage and benefit package exceeded union standards—without employees paying those pesky, needless dues. I'd like to think that we treated everybody respectfully, compassionately, professionally; that was our intention. The net: the vote to unionize fell well short. Then we fired all the rabble-rousers. Kidding—no reprisals, honest. We weren't tempted, and we also weren't stupid. The Labor Commission would have handed us our heads on a platter.

When he retired from his union, following his long run, Teamster leaders gathered for a big send-off in Oakland. He himself was left speechless, literally, at the celebration. By which I mean Popey stood up to the podium and could not utter a single world, not one. But the crowd cheered for him nonetheless. He was embraced by his colleagues, and sincerely. And he was loved by many, including his longtime and long-suffering administrative assistant. Janine was genuinely bereaved when I informed her of his passing. She sent a beautiful and impressive wreath for his memorial and sat in her pew teary-eyed throughout the services.

ORGANIZED CRIME?

I n 1993, in his capacity as a union official, my dad fell under the dreaded scrutiny of the FBI Strike Force. They were vigorously probing union corruption and the connection to organized crime. Nobody was under the illusion for a second that when Teamster President Jimmy Hoffa disappeared, he went underground to join an ashram in Nepal; more like under the ground of the football stadium then under construction in the Meadowlands.

The Freedom of Information and Privacy Act permitted me to initiate a general inquiry as to my father's criminal life—not that I knew anything about the FBI Strike Force interest in him. I conjectured it was worth a shot to see what I could see about his past, and that's where I first found out about it. Eleven months after my first formal request for information, I received eighty printed pages in his file.

The records indicated that the FBI had indeed staked him out. They were looking into the possibilities of his swinging sweetheart deals and taking in something like $500 a month under the table, trivial stakes considering the high risk. Notes refer to him as a former numbers runner in Brooklyn, and indicate that he went to the track every day, and that his son, my younger brother, was… At which point the notes were inscrutably redacted, but no doubt they indicated my brother was a drug addict and a felon, but why this information mattered here was left unexplained. The pages were heavily redacted elsewhere, too, and they would also not send me ten more pages existing in his file on the grounds that these contained information as to confidential procedures and identification.

When all was said and done, months later, my dad would be in the clear. As explained in a March 3, 1993, internal memo to the director, re: JOSEPH DI PRISCO, the FBI investigation "has revealed no specific evidence of criminal activity based upon these allegations [of a 'sweetheart' deal between union officials and employer representatives]. Investigation has shown evidence of possible misrepresentation to union members involving coverage of benefits. Information regarding this possible misrepresentation has been forwarded to the U.S. Department of Labor.

"On March 2, 1993, Assistant United States Attorney GEOFFREY A. ANDERSON declined prosecution in this matter. For this reason, the San Francisco Division is placing this matter in a 'Closed' status."

⟿

I MYSELF HAVE BEEN THE subject of a federal racketeering investigation. Actually I was identified as the prime suspect, formally advised by an FBI agent not to leave town, my phone tapped, my meetings covertly filmed, the whole deal. In case you're wondering, being branded the prime suspect in a Racketeer Influenced and Corrupt Organization Act investigation is not something you would put on your bucket list. My own lawyer advised the Bureau they were on a RICO fishing expedition. Lawyers voice such a cliché to the feds, and in my case it was true. Probably. We never really understood what they were looking for, and our requests for clarification were met with the default position: "All in due time," which meant, "wait till discovery." We had a few guesses—having to do with my connections with people who they probably believed were mobsters, and my involvement in business ventures, restaurants specifically, in which men of Italian descent went after each other, in the courts and elsewhere. My entrepreneurial associates and friends weren't mobsters, not really. Considering their various enterprises and all the vowels in their names, it was vaguely plausible to speculate as much, I suppose. But that I was the button in a racketeering operation? Wow, that was most surely insanely implausible. All they had to do was look into my financial assets or slice open my lumpy mattress to determine conclusively I was no big fish—but the skinniest sardine in the sea. Come to think of it, they did look into my finances, and evidently shared the numbers with people they interviewed—or so I was told by my brother, whom they interviewed.

I have been attempting for years to gain access to my own FOIA files, so far without success. But I will soldier on till I do. Seems overwhelmingly likely the FBI was intending to leverage me, to use me against my associates and to pressure me to flip on them—about what? I would like to know what their theory was. Hey, they surely knew my father's confidential informant past, so I guess it was worth a shot.

My case was eventually dropped as well, for reasons they never explained, and not before the scrutiny shredded my life for about a year. All that time, I was an anxious mess. One thing you never want is the feds investigating you—or, as the old man would delicately phrase it, *up your ass*. DOJ resources are effectively infinite, and nobody is innocent of everything, including me—and with all due *you know*, probably including you, whoever you are.

Also as it happened, the special agent in charge, the one who told me to stick around and not take any trips, interviewed my father about *my* activities. Talk about a switch I couldn't have anticipated.

In advance of that interview, I had briefed him a little bit, not that there was much I cared to reveal, but he himself didn't care to know too much, pure Brooklyn, pure plausibly deniable Pope. Afterward in our postmortem of the interview, he said it went all right, and he didn't have anything to tell the guy. I wished I could have been a fly on the wall to hear his non-responsive, passive-aggressive answers to the fed's queries.

How my father fared, emotionally and psychologically, during his own Strike Force investigation I will never know—which I guess applies to many other stages of his life. It's hard to imagine it didn't take its toll. Either that, or he had the mud to withstand the onslaught. Of course, I never knew about that investigation into him until shortly before he passed and his dementia took hold. In his lifetime, he never once said a word to me about the episode. In my dad's eyes, and as far as his son was concerned, it never happened. Who wantsta know?

Sympathy for the Guy Sitting On My Phone Tap

PLEASURES OF BEING THE PRIME SUSPECT

Not that I have much sympathy for him, but what was it like for the poor mope listening to my takeout Chinese orders, baby-talking girlfriend, screaming matches with you-know-who, my parents complaining about something and everything, and the meets with customers who needed product before the party?

I'm not admitting anything. What's to admit?

Lawsuits flying. Fists flying in the restaurant.

Getting fired as the general manager. Going to the hospital for stitches after a kitchen brawl.

Italians as restaurant business partners not getting along, on a hair trigger, ready to blow it all up. What could possibly go wrong?

Say that somebody was dealing, that he was using, that he was going through the seven-year-long breakup he confused with being in love.

Say that he was hanging by his fingernails in grad school, supposedly working on a Ph.D.

Say that the prime backer of his blackjack career was fat city, with too much free money not to take a flyer on new restaurants. Say that one night the man's brother-in-law broke into the Nob Hill apartment, pissed off about everything including not being respected or taken seriously and he'd show everybody what being taken seriously meant, and he tied up the backer's teenage daughter on a chair and lay in wait for him, and when he came home, he jumped him armed with a billy and they beat each other bloody, crashing all the way down the stairs and through the door and into the street, and the neighbors called the cops, and the brother-in-law did eighteen years for attempted murder and kidnapping.

But now say serious money was financially involved in that beautiful, new waterfront restaurant, where his partner told him to fuck off and stay out. Say that the judge was going to rule whether or not the business would go into receivership, pissing off everybody. Well, wouldn't it be good to show that the business partner, who had invested everything he had into the operation, didn't know how to run it? Who cared if it cost money in the short term, it was the long term that mattered. So it would be good to have it demonstrated to the judge that the restaurant's assets were being mismanaged. How to do that? Show decreasing receipts. How to decrease receipts? Bring the business to a halt, that's how. Flood the house with deadbeat patrons, recruited from the newspaper ads run for the purposes of doing a sociological study. Meet the unwitting participants week after week at a hotel near the waterfront, pay them cash to sit at their tables and order little or nothing. Then please fill out the study as to workplace attitudes of employees under stress. Also have somebody's father and brother hand out phony discount coupons to the restaurant, cause a little chaos on the floor. The local television nightly news reports on the scam, they mention the freebie offer comes courtesy of some fabricated entity known as The Friends of San Francisco. So what if the ace celebrity investigative reporter calls from the newspaper, wanting to ask a few questions? Somebody says, I have admired your work, which was true, though not in the moment. And then the FBI gets in touch with some information. Tells somebody he's a racketeer. He hires lawyers, sure, and wait…

Well, what somebody does is, he does the same so-called study at a restaurant solely owned by his backer. Totally legitimate, right? Suck on that, figure that one out. They film his meetings.

Somebody throws out the typewriters and all the survey materials. What study?

Not that any of that happened, of course.

Because that would be really crazy, wouldn't it? Who would believe it? Who would call that racketeering?

New York State Appellate Division

RECORDS AND BRIEFS

Q. *All right, now, did you call—call anyone in the City of New York and suggest that you would be willing to come back and testify in certain cases here?*

A. *No.*

Q. *Did anyone in the City of New York call you and ask you if you would testify in certain cases here?*

A. *No, sir.*

Q. *When you came back you made—you came back—*

JUDGE: *Did anybody talk to you and ask you if you would be willing to testify in certain cases?*

A. *In California?*

JUDGE: *Anywhere?*

A. *In California, I talked to nobody.*

Q. *Anywhere, his Honor asked you?*

A. *I didn't talk—*

Q. *(Interrrupting) Here, here in New York?*

A. *Oh, in New York?*

Q. *Yes?*

A. *Then if what, if I—*

Q. *(Interrupting) Anybody asked you, you would be willing to testify in certain cases here?*

A. *No, I—I—I spoke to the District Attorney, and he asked me [sic] cooperation, but told me I would be given consideration for my full cooperation.*

Exhibit D to Return

RESPONDENT'S CASE

The respondent did not testify in his own defense. Nor did he call any witnesses in his behalf. However, defense counsel stated in open court that the respondent would take the stand if he were called by the Department. The prosecution elected not to question him.

FINDINGS AND CONCLUSIONS

A. *Concerning the specification that respondent Celentano on certain occasions, without just cause, knowingly associated and had dealings with Joseph DiPrisco, a known criminal, gambler and person engaged in unlawful activities, not in the discharge of official duty and without the permission of the police commissioner. (Specification 1)*

The testimony of Joseph DiPrisco is controlling in the consideration of Specification 1. That specification in substance charges that the respondent on certain occasions associated and had dealings with DiPrisco who was a known criminal, gambler and person engaged in unlawful activities and that said association was without just cause, was without the permission of the Police Commissioner and was not in the discharge of respondent's official duties. I find that respondent is guilty of this specification.

DiPrisco testified that he was a police informant, for which service he expected to and did receive sums of money from the police officers to whom he funneled tips and leads. Among these police officers were the respondent and one Patrolman Vincent (Jimmy) Santa. On occasions the information he furnished resulted in arrests. However, on other occasions, the scheme between these three conspirators consisted of DiPrisco furnishing information on a gambler or parole violator engaged in

MORNING BELLS ARE RINGING, MORNING BELLS ARE RINGING

A silk red-and-green paisley bathrobe hangs upstairs in my closet. The label indicates it is from a tony department store. I don't wear the garment. I haven't worn it since—I cannot remember, could be twenty-five years, maybe more. I didn't plan to wear it when I got it. People who organize other people's lives and possessions for a living play a useful role, no doubt, but I will never hire them. I have a friend who does this professionally, but as much as I like her, I won't retain her services. I might read organizers' blogs, I might read their books, for the vicarious kick of feeling another's endorphin rush before the spectacle of pristine closets and liberated shoe racks. I know if you have not worn an article of clothing for a year, you're supposed to throw it out or recycle or donate. I would also say that probably the same principle applies to ideas you haven't used for a year. But my disorganized library, books

I haven't cracked open since college? You'd have to pry them from my cold, ink-stained, manicure-begging hands. In my defense, not that I'm bragging, when last we moved, I did donate nine or ten heavy boxes of books to assisted living centers. I am indeed a hoarder of sorts, but that's not the reason I am keeping the robe.

The reason is that my brother gave it to me, or he sold it to me, I cannot recall, but either is possible. I am fairly certain, and was fairly certain at the time he presented it to me, that he boosted it—that is, stole it from that swanky store on Union Square, San Francisco. I bet it had a pretty price tag, and it boggles my mind that he was able to navigate the aisles of merchandise and escape the clutches of department store security: no easy matter given how he looked at the time, ponytailed and scruffy and tweaking, wearing wraparound sunglasses and bandana.

Here's the problem. If I get rid of the robe, I would be ridding myself of a piece of my brother. But why would it be valuable to me, given that it attaches to his lowest point in life as a junkie stealing to support his habit? Mine is a fairly indefensible position, it could be argued. I can criticize myself for contributing to his addiction by implicitly or tacitly approving of his crime, and deriving personal gain—even if I hardly ever wore it and therefore never derived sartorial advantage. Indefensible it may be, but it's the position I am taking.

Trying to be a good brother to my jonesing little brother perennially shoved him and me into switches like that. I watched him when he kicked a couple of times. Not that it stuck for him, but the vomiting and the weeping and the groaning were nightmarish to behold during his withdrawal attempts. They say it's easier to suffer than to watch a loved one suffer, and that's true. But coming off smack? I don't know if I could do that. You say no all the time to a junkie, and push them away, because that's tough love, supposedly a sound tack. Tough love is easier digested via TV documentaries, I believe, not for people you really love. In my opinion, tough love, which the detox programs insist upon, is finally no love. I loved him and he infuriated me. He'd say the same, if for different reasons. I kept the robe and I keep it for the same reason I kept a few of his prison letters, because these things are all that remain, all the existing physical evidence he once was alive.

Here is where the story of my father converges, not only with my story, but with my brother John's.

∽

WHEN MY MOTHER LANDED on a notion or a turn of phrase she approved, like an Everglades gator with a dam-building beaver in its jaws, she never let go till she killed it. She repeatedly observed that my father and his son John were "two peas in a fuckin' pod." Her conclusion infuriated her husband, who typically sputtered with outrage whenever she threw the bombshell accusation over the psychic fortress walls my father lived behind. My brother was similarly offended; he wouldn't wish to be compared to his father, who, to him, was a liar and a con man, a chump and a loser who stole or borrowed money from him and never paid him back.

She had a point. Each was defined, each was eaten alive, by his own addiction beast. For my father, it was gambling. For my brother, smack. A simple, solid working definition of addiction: the compulsion to repeat injurious behavior despite being aware of the damage that is wreaked upon one's life. Two peas in a fucking pod indeed. If you add me, that would be three, and that would be the case for me at some point; more about that later.

∼

JOHN DID SERIOUS TIME in San Quentin and in Nevada State Prison, often in max; I estimate about ten years total. Inside, he was in and out of the hole, solitary confinement. He belonged at one stage to the Aryan Brotherhood, so he said, although he was no skinhead racist; he told me he needed to belong to a group to survive, and by his calculation he was outnumbered ten to one by the brothers in gen pop. He also claimed, when he was out of prison, some vague associate status with the Hells Angels, but I never understood what he meant. He had learned how to mix it up on the street as a teenager, long before he was sentenced, and he pumped up his body over the years, conditioning he couldn't maintain when he was mainlining and ravaging himself. He told me about the beatings that took place inside prison walls that nauseated him. He was arrested dozens of times: drug offenses, boosting from department stores, burglaries, that sort of thing, and his rap sheet goes on for thirty pages. Probably his most serious crime was the armed stickup of the restaurant where he used to be the manager. He got away with that one, yet despite his wearing a ski mask, we all knew, including the restaurant owner, that he was the button.

He was a heroin addict off and on, mostly on, for at least twenty-five years. He drove hog Harleys, he liked his dogs big and bruising, such as Dobermans and boxers, and he took care of them lovingly and they were loyal to him—and instinctively sweet to everybody in the family. Girls, and later women, unfailingly swooned around him. He married twice; once to a much younger and slippery biker babe, who struck me as being reliable as an under-the-overpass dime-bag dealer, and that union was over in a flash; the second time to an ex-junkie, a simpler, equally damaged and fairly good-hearted soul who loved him. They met in rehab and she had a teenage son, for whom John was a doting stepfather since the boy's father was in prison.

John was a charmer. He was funny, he was smart, he was sensitive, probably too sensitive. Every so often he would try to mend fences with his parents. My mother was all over the place on that subject, sometimes cursing him out, sometimes bailing him out, figuratively as well as financially. Junkies do that to people they care about. And on this score I cannot fault my mother. She was as confused as anybody, and she was his mother, and he was her baby, her youngest child, Johnny Cake, and she was continually devastated. My father's position was less nuanced. I heard him tell my brother many, many times: "Your credibility sucks." A constant refrain, admittedly not without foundation.

By any measure, the old man was right, John's credibility was— not. Like many a junkie, he had immense, practically unbounded capacities for deception, dissimulation, evasion. Whenever he worked me, for money, of course, always for money when not for a place to sleep or shower, he would spin elaborate stories and explanations. Whenever a story goes on too long, somebody is lying. Watchword for writers, too, now that I think about it. If you have ever had a friend or family member who is an addict, you know you spend a fair amount of time fending them off. They wear you out with their self-serving demands, their needs, their schemes, their rationalizations, their pleas for understanding, compassion, and cash. Everything ultimately boils down to a plea for money—and the need for money is as urgent as a heart attack, which, considering John's numerous mainline-heroin-related cardiac diseases, was not a long shot.

I'm on the OCD, that is, obsessive-compulsive, spectrum; to put it another way, I am absolutely non-ADD, I am hypervigilant, never permitting my attention to wander for a second—for if I did, the door would be unlocked, or the germs on my unwashed hands might kill me, or some other catastrophe would result from my failure to check and re-recheck the car, the oven, the front door, anything, everything.

On the other hand, John and my father were both ADD. Beyond that, they were both the black sheep in their families. My father was often roughed up by his own brutalizing old-world Italian father, who probably saw no way of dealing with his out-of-control son other than violence and tying him up in the cellar and leaving him to sleep on the floor in the dark. My brother and father threw fists at each other more than a couple of times, but the abuse Johnny felt he received was more psychological than physical. He never felt loved by his father. He often said as much in so many words. This didn't stop him from continually seeking out that love. As a practical matter, their attention spans rivaled a squirrel's. For instance, I never saw either of them with a book in their hands. They couldn't sit still, unless in front of a television set—and not with a cocktail in hand; neither of them really drank. In another age and if they were different people, I suppose medication would have been indicated. They both had the ability to seduce people, by which I mean strangers. My father had no genuinely close friends, as in somebody to go out with for a beer or to the game, and he was congenitally suspicious of others' motivations relative to him. Everybody's trying to clip you: words he lived by, possibly because they were not unrelated to his M.O. for working others. On the other hand, Johnny had many very loyal friends, to whom he was unfailingly generous, throughout the years of his addiction. Hundreds of heartbroken people showed up for his memorial service and wept for him.

Yes, Winnicott does have something to add; this is the concluding paragraph of his essay on "Aspects of Juvenile Delinquency":

"...if the child becomes able to manage himself and his relationship to grown-ups and to other children, he still has to begin dealing with complications, such as a mother who is depressed, a father with maniacal episodes... The more we think of these things the more we understand why infants and little children absolutely need the background of their own family, and if possible a stability of physical surroundings as well; and from such considerations we see that children deprived of home life must either be provided with something personal and stable when they are yet young enough to make use of it to some extent, or else they must force us later to provide stability in the shape of an approved school, or, in the last resort, four walls in the shape of a prison cell."

Winnicott is on to something. After all, I was the one who took refuge in a school, my little brother, in jail.

CORRESPONDENCES

A small number of letters between John and me have survived all the moves and depredations of time and circumstance. Precomputer, preemail, as this era was, I have a few of my brother's originals and, strangely, a couple of copies of my own letters. One of my missives qualifies as probably the longest letter I ever wrote in my life, about 2,800 words on ten yellow-line legal tablet pages. For some odd, to me, reason I thought to make and retain a carbon copy. It was dated April 14, 1980.

The voice is mine, I can tell, and it's by me in some early incarnation. At times, I come across a little bit preachy, if not sanctimonious—though I can also see that I am trying hard not to be: "I miss you, brother John. *I want you not to give up. I want you to clean up and use this time in prison.* Stop reading this if it sounds like bullshit to you." But then I really go off the rails: "If you're living in a hell, it's only another version of hell that most people live in every single day of their stinking, useless, rotten lives... *USE this time, don't do this time, don't let it do you.*" I wrote it, and I'm not proud of it.

I express my pained interest as to life inside. At the time I was a grad student, and I was under the influence of philosophers like Michel Foucault, who were all the rage in the academy I lamely aspired to inhabit. I might have been reading *Discipline and Punish: The Birth of the Prison*, which I thought brilliant. His insights into the panopticon and surveillance and the modern state system were provocative. But I was dealing with my brother, who knew the scoop firsthand.

Mostly, I am curious about *him* on the inside, and him before he was on the inside. As ever, I afflict him with a lot of questions:

It all seemed like whatever was happening to you was happening in the world you had been creating—for how long now? Months? Years? Since the time we were growing up in Brooklyn? Since the imaginative time you broke away from some thing—what was it?—the old man? Me? What I or everybody in our sick family represented? I don't know when it all began. I tend to think that it had something to do with Kit [his best friend killed before his eyes in a motorcycle crash], *or something to do with* [the restaurant where he was the manager], *or probably something to do with our father.*

Hey, did they tell you I tried to visit you a few weeks ago, on a Thursday? They wouldn't let me, it wasn't visiting days. Jerks. Barred. And then I got barred at the Park Tahoe. I was using Revere [a card-counting system]—*not badly either but, damn it, the same pit boss that barred me at Caesar's Palace in Vegas must have recalled me, because right after he noticed me I got the heave ho. The guy goes, "Please take this as a compliment, sir. You are an excellent 21 player, please don't come here anymore." Idiots.*

I will start writing to you very often if you want me to, & I hope that you do. Please write back soon, since I worry for you & care very much for you.

With love,

Your brother

〜

JOHN'S LETTER FROM NEVADA State Prison, Carson City, Nevada; found inside an envelope postmarked 20 August 1980; composed by hand on lined paper, the cursive elegant; as with all his missives quoted below, usually no paragraph breaks and no margins, each page numbered consecutively at the top; spelling and punctuation are, as they appear below, various and inconsistent. He is weeks away from his twenty-ninth birthday. Other letters quoted below are from San Quentin or Santa Rita Jail.

Brother Joe,

Hows life in the fast lane? I got your letter. Its been the same old grind in the place. I havent been going to work lately. I guess my attitude has been bad. But I take as much shit as I can take from these pork chop eating mother fucken police. My close friend got stuck yesterday he aint hurt too bad Both his lungs got punctured. But they say he will be short winded for a while but will soon be good as new. He aint saying who hit him so it must be personal. I dont know who did it or I'd be knocking at his door myself. I cant say anymore about that cause I dont know if the crazy police read my mail or not. Hey, Brother Im gonna go to the Chow Hall right now I'll be back in a flash OK! Here I am back to say the food stunk. Brother Joe this place is getting on my nerves. I am trying to keep my sanity but it goes deeper than you could imagine. Hey enough of that talk. I won a T.V. in a poker game a few days ago so the time has been better for me at night. Now I can watch my own tube. I scored a radio and head phone 2 weeks ago So I guess you could say Im cadillacing or other words living it up. What a joke Huh? Right now Im listening to the Rolling Stones singing emotional rescue. Last night I watched that show about Rock + Roll. It was pretty good. I guess your wondering how Im scoring these luxuries. Me and a couple paissanos are running a black jack game Prison style. The house turns both cards up and the house wins pushes. You cant help but take everybody for what they got. So far things have been good anyway. We started backing the game on

our ass (NO BANKROLL) but if someone would have stuck us for any
bread I would have been all about boxing for it. But since then were in
OK shape on the bread side. Well big Brother I love ya and miss you Say
hello Father Shane for me OK

Love,

John

∽

POSTMARKED THE SAME DAY as that letter to me, there is another communication of his, not to me, but to our favorite very bad girl, the charismatic and sexy Sandy. She had her own drug and alcohol problems starting from early adolescence and was in and out of prison herself. The reason this letter is in my possession is that my father photocopied some of it and mailed it to me. How he came upon it, I have no information or recollection. But my father's objective is transparent enough. He wanted me to see how incorrigible John was; the proof, to him, was found in his letter to Sandy. If someone wanted to make that case, John's words furnished support. There are numerous unreadable passages, and his ragged state of mind might have contributed to the unintelligibility.

Hey girl what's going on? I got your letter today. I'm glad to see that
your heart is back where it should be. Ha! So your fuckin up a little.
Hey don't let it get you down. I 'm in prison and I say to myself that

when I get out I'm going to be clean. But I 'm fixing every day in this mother fucken place. I don't want to tell anybody that but I'm telling you because so what if [illegible] will is a little weak that don't make you a bad person and fuck [illegible] in the neck if they hassle you in your life and you should want [illegible] Sandy Im not gonna lie to you or to myself. But Im always going to go and get loaded. Im gonna get [illegible]to get strung out and I probably will get strung. If that was the case I wont last long and I know it. got to put your mind over your [illegible] desires. I always did pretty good. I could chip with the best of them... I'm gonna get out of this place cause believe me Sandy this place aint where its at. Looking forward to spending time with you when I get out. Who knows maybe we do eachother good. Wow! I know [illegible] but you got to keep an agreement with me and that is you promise me stay out of jail. That would be crazy if I get out and you get slammed [illegible]. OK sweetheart Im gonna get this letter to you. Take care of yourself.

Love,

John

∽

Saturday, 9/27/80

Brother Joe, Hey Whats going on? I got myself in some trouble brother. I am sitting in the hole right now. I went to court yesterday. Its a disciplinary court. No matter what your charged with your *automatically found guilty cause these police sit on the board as judges. Well anyway I got charged with disobeying a direct order, obstructing a search, and assault on an officer. I was found guilty and Monday they are transporting me over to Max. I think this probably is going to fuck up my parole but What can I say its over and done with now. Your probably wondering What happened Well I wake up it was Sunday morning All I had on was my bathrobe. I was walking down from one tier to another wing when these two bulls stopped me and asked what was under my robe I told them nothing but a big dick. Anyhow a human being can only take so much brother It comes to point when you are pushed up against a wall and your tired of getting shaken down, searched 10 times a day. You can only take so much humiliation and I guess I felt I ate enough humble pie. So as I said I didnt have any clothes on underneath. So I was not going to stoop to thier silly little game. I told them that if they wanted to search me we could go back to my area and search me there at my house No they insisted on doing it right there so that 30 other people could see them play their game. The deciding point that got me mad was they said If I didnt take off the robe that we are going to rip it off you B-O-Y! I guess I hate being called a boy and I wasn't going to be humiliated anymore. So I started walking back down to my hose they these two red neck fat crew cutted pork chop eating no good dogs jumped on me. One guy grabbed my hair and another twisted my arm to make a long story short I dropped both of them with a couple of assorted kicks and went down to my pad. Sure enough the goon squad came all 15 of them handcuffed me and leg shackled me and drug me over to the hole. When I was in the hole where none could see they kicked me in the stomach around 20 or 30 times I dont know exactly cause I couldnt breathe and that's the end of the story. Im OK now my ribs feel pretty bangedup but other than that Im OK...*

It would be good if I could get the Old Man to write [a letter to the Parole Board] for me but I wouldnt ask him in a million years. But the main letter is from you Joe about me having a place to live. Look at it this way If I dont get paroled at least we all tried. OK! I personally think you would have done the same thing I did with these punk police. Im just tired, tired, tired of their fucken mickey mouse bullshit. Well anyway. OK Brother. Remember. Im gonna get out sooner or later so dont feel bad if they dump me at the parole board.

Love,

John

PS these punk police confiscated my TV and stereo because when they rolled up all my property they claimed that a TV and stereo were never mailed to me and therefore if it wasn't mailed to directly from an appliance store that it was now considered an unauthorized item end of story FUCK THEM PUNKS

I have no recollection of his being paroled around this time, but it's possible.

∾

Wend. Oct, 15

Brother Joe, You ask me What movie do I think I'm in. Well have you ever seen seen the movie Cool Hand Luke with Paul Newman, it shows the way of prison life and how bad the porkers treat convicts. I aint trying to copy no movie or actor. And I aint going to snivel about how bad the conditions are here in prison its very obvious that they are fucked. But What I will say about my situation on how I got here was because of drugs...

Its hard for me to explain to you all the things I feel Joe. But I sure have been doing a great amount of thinking lately. I sincerely wish I could leave this whole farce behind me and be able to be on the streets to try and earn some respect and promise some good results and get something more out of life than What I'm experiencing here. I love you Joe and appreciate everything youve done for me.

John

∾

FROM A LETTER POSTMARKED 21 September 1981, Alameda County Jail, Santa Rita:

Friday, Night

Brother Joe,

Hey I guess your pretty well fed up with me. I can say Im fed up with myself But Im also ready to cut the whole family loose, only cause I dont want to hurt anybody anymore. This drug program is my last chance and I know it. I would be lying to you if I told you I didn't need some professional help. Heroin is the boss. Its too strong a temptation for me. I aint going to sit here and snivel to you. Im an asshole for not being strong enough to overcome it by myself. Its other people who sit in their high positions and look down at me for being addicted to a narcotic. Hey If I become famous some day I can say that I too was a once addicted drug addict. But my problem sure aint the lone ranger either. and I won't be the first one who has gone to a drug program and failed and I am going to try and put all my energy behind getting clean, and If I dont I havent hurt anyone but my-self. I guarantee you that big brother. You got to excuse me for having a bad attitude cause I certainly do have one at the present time. You dont seem to understand the problem is bigger than the world seems to you, and until I've got it under control and have had time to mentally overcome my desire for stuff I aint changed a bit. And at this point I need to get into a drug program quick fast and in a hurry. Prisons, jails, are the biggest backbone and thriver of dope phenes. This aint whats happening here at Santa Rita. Im eligible on Nov. 18th as long as Nevada drops its hold on me…

[He goes into intricate detail on the pending proceedings in various jurisdictions, and expresses the hope to get into drug diversion.]

Once I make bail I go directly into the custody of Walden House. So Brother Joe there is a whole lot at stake for me and Im still really up in the air about where I actually stand. I'll try contacting you in the next week or two I sure would like you to come and visit me Michelle comes up once a week. OK Big Brother I send my love to Mario.

John

I never did visit him in Santa Rita. He was eventually released to a program. The court appearances, the bail hearings, the conferences with drug counselors, the prison visits, the refusals to visit San Quentin, the collect phone calls from inside—it's all jumbled in my head, all these markers and events blend. The years of waiting for something positive to happen wore me down, and I had problems of my own to confront. That's not a defense, merely my miserable explanation.

∾

THIS IS FROM A nine-page letter of unknown origins and date; internal clues suggest it could be from San Quentin:

Friday 18,

Brother Joe,

Hey well you know I wasnt mad at you. But I certainly wasnt going to write to you until I first got a letter from you. But by God I got your letter today So here I am writing to my big brother. Seriously it was good hear from you. That's too bad that you got barred from that casino. You know we got one thing in common I got barred from the streets. You know brother Joe these jails and prisons seem to be 20 years behind the times. [He details black and white violence inside the prison, and his frequent fights.] *If they know your a crazy white boy they arent going to keep fucking with you. I guess your probably thinking to yourself Joe that there has got to be another more sensible way to stay out of trouble. Yeah there is. I can go and tell the bull that I want protective custody (PC) and they will take me and lock me up with all the misfits and perverts and mother fuckers. No Brother Joe I'll hang in there and I'm going to walk this prison yard and come and go as I please until my parole date and then Ill get out of this mother fucken place. I know you would understand my position better if you were to see these conditions for yourself. So try and get off that crazy subject. I have been staying in good shape I weigh about 180 and have been working out everyday. You know I have been learning alot of karate while I have been in jail…I'd be more than happy to show you everything I know I'm gonna learn. In the last letter I got from Roberta included inside was a couple of space ships that Mario had drawn. They were real nice…You asked me if I would like to read that book by Norman Mailer.* [I believe it must have been *The Executioner's Song.*] *Yes I would… Since I am out in the middle of the desert It gets pretty hot and that sun is overbearing I could definitely use a good pair of sunglasses preferably Ray Bann (Aviator Style) the kind with the plastic forhead guard and the cable that looks around your ear… But I would appreciate some good novels to read. You dont*

have to go out and buy any just send some of the ones you already have.
Also in your letter you asked about my sentence. I got 4 years... Maybe
the Old Man could work something out for me [once I get paroled]. Well
Brother Joe. I'm gonna get this letter in the mail. Say hello to Father
Shane for me... Thanks Again, Big Brother

Your baby brother
John

✐

FATHER SHANE, THESE DAYS a Catholic priest for fifty years and a
monsignor, once visited him in Nevada State Prison, wearing his
blacks with Roman collar. He said it was an unremittingly scary
place, but John made him feel welcome and safe. Shane was trained
as a psychotherapist, and he always liked him. As the priest said, my
brother looked like a bad ass but he could not hide the little boy inside.

John battled the typical grave junkie diseases: pericarditis,
endocaritis, phlebitis. His scabbed legs and arms resembled moonscape.
He did two or three stints at various stages of his addiction in Walden
House, San Francisco, a drug diversion program. It was a tough
love, no bullshit sort of operation, and he cleaned up for stretches,
and he cultivated strong connections with a couple of well-meaning
counselors, who hung with him, never giving in to his crap, but also
never giving up hope for him. This is the hard line anybody who ever

loved him walked at one point or another. His greatest advocate, and his friend, was the magnetic director Alfonso Acampora.

2003-03-25 San Francisco—The apparent suicide of Walden House CEO Alfonso Acampora came as his leadership at the nationally renowned drug and alcohol rehabilitation program was under threat from a state attorney general's investigation into alleged financial irregularities.

The criminal probe, which has been under way for six months, was prompted by a whistleblower complaint from a former Walden House board member who has alleged widespread fiscal mismanagement at the nonprofit. The complaint included allegations that Acampora padded the payroll with family members, doled out business to members of the Walden House board and billed the agency for his own questionable and sometimes lavish perks.

—sfgate.com

⌐

I find it difficult to read much less understand prison memoirs. Perhaps the material is too hot for me. Once at Cal I taught Jack Henry Abbott's *In the Belly of the Beast*, but I don't think I ever got emotionally past what the man did upon being released, that is, stabbing to death a waiter he felt had disrespected him. People are still talking about Piper Kerman's *Orange Is the New Black*, and her story truly makes for terrific television. Then there's also Joe Loya, a onetime bank robber, who writes powerfully and authentically of his time behind bars without excusing himself.

For my money, nobody compares to Dietrich Bonhoeffer, a genuinely heroic man who was imprisoned and executed at thirty-nine for resisting the Nazis. A trailblazing theologian and pastor, he wrote heartbreakingly clarion prose, including these words from his great *Letters and Papers from Prison*:

We must learn to regard people less in the light of what they do or omit to do, and more in the light of what they suffer...

There is nothing that can replace the absence of someone dear to us, and one should not even attempt to do so. One must simply hold out and endure it. At first that sounds very hard, but at the same time it is also a great comfort. For to the extent the emptiness truly remains unfilled one remains connected to the other person through it. It is wrong to say that God fills the emptiness. God in no way fills it but much more leaves it precisely unfilled and thus helps us preserve—even in pain— the authentic relationship. Furthermore, the more beautiful and full the remembrances, the more difficult the separation. But gratitude transforms the torment of memory into silent joy. One bears what was

lovely in the past not as a thorn but as a precious gift deep within, a
hidden treasure of which one can always be certain.

This speaks to me about my brother.

～

Nobody is going to argue that prison in the United States is a
path to rehabilitation. To be clear, of course the community is
probably safer for the incarceration of hardened criminals. But just
as obviously, prisons are overcrowded with low-level drug offenders,
banished there due to the minimum sentencing madness of the
eighties, prisoners who are easy pickings for the gangs who fearlessly
roam the yard.

Yes, prison writings make for a distinct, often potent genre. The
problem with reading my brother's letters is they don't read like a genre
to me. My brother is part of no genre, he is sui generis. His words are
the only words left that belong to him. As I pore over these letters,
John's indignation feels real, his agony palpable. His voice is alive.
His words curl around in my head like the omnipresent concertina
wire above his prison walls, every bit as entangling, as restraining,
as wounding.

What is the purpose of a memoir? Or this memoir? Is it to exhume
the memories? Is it to bring back the dead? Is it to make sure the living
never perish? If so, it's a doomed project. That doesn't mean it must
be a failure. People die, their stories do not. And their pain persists as

well, but as it was when they were alive we can do very little to assuage that unassuageable pain.

Reading my brother's letters rocks me decades after he penned them. He's fixing every day, I have to assume, and he's fucked up, and playing me, and he is hopeless, but since he was once alive, maybe he isn't hopeless, and he feels alive. Which he always will be.

At the same time, I will always fail him because he will never be here in the world again.

If Bonhoeffer is right, I should regard John in the light of all he suffered.

Ghosts. I don't believe in them. But sometimes they seem to believe in me.

He was hospitalized at least three times I am aware of, not counting prison infirmaries. At least once I was there on his death watch at Highland Hospital in Oakland, a death that didn't materialize then, or during his other hospital stays. His death occurred later, when he OD'd and died, alone on the tiled bathroom floor of his San Francisco apartment. Coroner's terse determination: acute drug toxicity. He was fifty-one years old.

There is nothing that can replace the absence of someone dear to us, and one should not even attempt to do so. One must simply hold out and endure it. At first that sounds very hard, but at the same time it is also a great comfort.

〜

THIS IS WHAT I said on January 25, 2003, to the almost two hundred people who had gathered to say goodbye to Johnny:

In times of mourning people speak of how someone touched their lives. I understand what they mean, but Johnny did more than touch our lives.

Johnny was a storm. Johnny is a storm. A storm of truths, a storm of confusion. A storm of rose petals, a storm of steel. A nonviolent man who was a man of violent self-contradictions. A man who infuriated us, a man who made us laugh. A man we wanted to scream at, a man we wanted to put in our pocket for safekeeping.

I guess this is a way to say that he was a human being with his weaknesses and his strengths. With weaknesses and vulnerabilities that were his strengths.

So I have one intention here today. To honor my little brother Johnny by being as honest as I can be about him. And if I can, to speak a few words that wouldn't embarrass him too much.

I can't speak for the Johnny you knew—the Johnny you gave birth to, or were married to, or loved, or rode with, or worked with—the Johnny you cherish and miss so much today. I'm not sure I can really speak for the Johnny I think I knew. There were so many Johnnys.

Thousands of years ago somebody wrote a book that is read by millions of people everyday. It is one of the most famous books of all time and it ends like this: "But there were many other things which he did; if every one of them were written down, I suppose that the world itself could not contain the books that would be written."

That book has a title that is very fitting. You will find it in the Bible. It is called the Gospel According to John.

The world cannot contain all the stories that could be told: The Gospel According to Johnny. There were many Johnnys. Maybe too many Johnnys. Some of them were hard to take, some of them too beautiful to be believed. I don't know everything you know, but I know there were Johnnys you never knew, just as there were Johnnys I never knew.

Still, I myself can only begin by remembering the good times, the hilarious times, the sweet times. His great dogs—Thomson and Renzo. His Harleys. His generous Christmas presents. Trips to Tahoe. Thanksgiving Dinners. Working at Giovanni's—where John was easily the best restaurant manager you could imagine. And what a cook and bartender and waiter. The best. And the football games. Blackjack. The parties. More than anything, the heartbreaking kindnesses he routinely performed for all of us.

If he was your waiter—at Scoma's, at Eugene's—you would have given him a 30 percent tip or more—and asked for him the next time you came to the restaurant. If you were his nephew and two years old, like Mario once was, he would have put a big Raiders hat on your little head and big leather gloves on your tiny hands and set you on his Harley *where you would be beaming with joy about being lucky enough to have him for your uncle. If you were any one of his loyal dogs, you would protect him against anything and everyone. If you met him when he was straight, which he was for eight precious years, he spoke to you from his heart and made you feel that you mattered—and you never walked away from him without knowing you had been in a rare presence. If you were his tapped-out graduate student older brother, like I was in 1975, he would have gotten you a job so you could pay the bills. And if you were his brother at five years old and fifteen months older than Johnny, as I was, you would be—I can see it now—side by side on the couch watching with hushed breath* The Wizard of Oz *and hoping along with him for a happy ending somewhere over the rainbow.*

Yes, a happy ending. I'm still hoping for John to have a happy ending. And as an old friend of his, Father Shane, said, "When I think of Johnny I see a beautiful wild stallion." And then he added that Johnny is now enjoying his greatest thrill—the greatest high of all—in heaven, where his sufferings are now fulfilled.

But I need to remember how much John suffered—and in ways I will never completely understand.

Yes, a man of contradictions.

We knew this day would happen, and that it would come too soon, as it did. And as clearly as we knew it, we still cannot believe it. Johnny broke our hearts while he was alive, he is breaking our hearts now that he is not. We are helpless before this experience—but maybe not.

Maybe not. Maybe Johnny is leading us, but the problem is I can't tell where. To be honest, I never knew where he was leading me when he was alive. Maybe there's a chance he is leading me to a little bit of wisdom, maybe to a measure of peace. If you're like me, you could use a lot of both right now.

In Psalm 139, I find something I can use. This is the song that begins, "Lord, thou hast examined me and knowest me. Thou knowest all, whether I sit down or rise up." And he goes on: "Where can I escape from thy spirit? Where can I flee from thy presence?"

It's an interesting question, and a strange one. I mean, why would someone want to flee from his presence, to flee from being known?

But the answer is obvious. We all want to escape. Life is hard. We live in a vale of tears. And yet, of course, we also live in a world of wonders. What an ordinary contradiction.

Here's another one. We know we must die. Yet we find the idea personally incredible—how can we possibly die? So what is it? Are we crazy? Or are we immortal? Or are we both crazy and immortal?

Reason I mention this: Doesn't that sound like Johnny? Crazy and immortal. Crazily immortal. Immortally crazy.

Johnny is all-too-human. He wanted escape—but he also wanted freedom and a new life.

Let's go back to Psalm 139: feeling sad and confused, the speaker in the psalm comes to an insight:

"If I say, Surely darkness will steal over me,

[and] night will close around me,

darkness is no darkness for thee

and night is luminous as day;

to thee both dark and light are one."

To God both dark and light are one. To God both dark and light are one.

That's the sort of God who will welcome with open arms Johnny, a man of self-contradictions, a man acquainted equally with the light and the dark.

I believe that Johnny did the heroic best he could with his life. And the best he could is far better than most of us can contemplate.

We can lament the loss of everything that Johnny was, but let us not stop there. When we are honest with ourselves—when I am honest with myself—I know the existence of the deepest darkness even in the most dazzling light. And I know—I believe—I hope—I trust—that for Johnny that darkness somehow right now is shining with an unimaginable light. He was and is a world of wonders unto himself.

When Johnny telephoned my office or house, he would guess sometimes I would be screening my calls, and he always rambled and rambled on and on till I picked up: "Brother Joe, pick up the phone. It's your brother John. Brother Joe, pick up the phone."

Brother John, I don't know how this happened, but I'm still here.

New York State Appellate Division

RECORDS AND BRIEFS

Q. *You are presently under arrest under a warrant charging you with forgery in Brooklyn, is that right?*

A. *I guess so.*

Q. *You guess so?*

A. *Well, I'm here.*

[Flurry of objections.]

Q. *What do you mean when you say, "I'm here"?*

A. *Well, I didn't mean anything by it as far as that goes.*

Q. *Well as a matter of fact where were you arrested?*

[More objections.]

[Counsel for accused police officer]: Your Honor, it is not a question which will tend to incriminate or degrade him.

[Presiding]: If it was outside the state you know as well as I do, that flight is an indication of guilt.

[Counsel for accused police officer]: If Your Honor please, if he's arrested outside the city, he could be here for a perfectly valid reason, I don't say he fled, maybe he says it, I don't say it.

[Presiding]: I don't see how it is material as why he was—where he was arrested?

[Counsel for accused police officer]: As to why he's brought back here, he is testifying here for a particular purpose, I want to show the purpose.

…

Q. *You were arrested in California, weren't you?*

[Objections, rulings.]

[Presiding]: Anything that pertains to the particular act, flight after the commission of a crime is an indication of guilt and if the witness—I'm sorry [Counselor], you and I disagree, I will not order him to answer.

[Objections, rulings.]

[Counsel for accused police officer]: I say the question as to whether he called the State of New York to bring—that he was in California—to come back to New York, is not tending to incriminate or degrade him. Voluntary submission to arrest doesn't tend to incriminate or degrade you.

[Presiding]: I have already ruled on it.

[Counsel for accused police officer]: On what?

[Presiding]: I refuse to direct him to answer the question.

Mysteries of the (Hair) Salon

Long, long ago a fast-talking, lookame, bodybuilding, slicked-back, tank-topped Jersey Boy was the hairdresser of a serious girlfriend of mine in California. She was a highly entertaining companion for a spell, then a highly disastrous one after our relationship foundered. As the sages of Brooklyn might wisely weigh in, *Whaddaya gonna do?* I'm not implying I was capable of being philosophical about the turn in my romantic fortunes at the time, because I have never been philosophical when it comes to such turns. It's too late, but now this whole salon sex derby setup sounds partway toward a viable reality TV show pitch. (Showtime, Netflix, HBO, whoever, have your people call my people.)

Somewhere in the intermediate stage of this romance, or whatever the term for our connection, she told me she had a problem with Jersey Boy. No, he was a terrific hairdresser, whatever that meant, so that wasn't the problem. It seems that he had been down on his luck and had been in need of a few bucks. She lent him $200. (We are talking around 1980, about $600 in today's dollars.) She was a student, so this was not an easily write-offable number for her.

Why the fuck did you lend this clown money in the first place? I must have tenderly sympathized, and she must have defended herself, and her explanation must have pivoted upon the persuasiveness of his Jersey Boy sob story and hinged upon his trustworthy pledge to pay it back soon, and she told me the truth because this was before she became bad news. I must have assumed he was not making a play for her. One, because, being an idiot, I probably assumed he was gay, since of course all male hairdressers were, despite the evidence mounted and mounted again in Warren Beatty's *Shampoo*, which was a great movie in the theaters then and proving the opposite; and Two, how does a man's liquidity challenge factor into a viable seduction trap? You can see how the mind of a man like me was working, or mostly wasn't. In any case, the poser's note was way past due, and she was strapped. I would see what I could do about it.

I know. I'm a prince, right? If she needed some cash to buy groceries or something nice to wear or books for her classes, I would take care of it, because I was doing all right at the time, but that wasn't the point. It was the principle. Nowadays, when I hear somebody say, *It's not the money, it's the damn principle,* I always think, *No, it's always the damn money.* Much more to the point, somebody—some guy—was ripping off my girlfriend, and therefore some guy was disrespecting *me*. The things a man will do for love of a woman, or love of himself. It doesn't come close to the insane things he does to maintain his own precious illusions of respectability.

This sad and silly episode takes us back to Berkeley, the land that shining disco balls and *Saturday Night Fever* forgot, and before I was thirty. That is when I assumed solving problems for a pretty girl was a surefire route to her heart. Or some other, more desirable place. I have reason to believe that if I had read some columns in the women's magazines littering Jersey Boy's hair salon, I would have learned that women didn't really want a man to try to solve their problems, and when was the last time in recorded history that a guy ever got some action by trying to solve a girl's problem? Instead, when women related their problems, the advice columnists counseled, they wanted to be heard out empathetically, they wanted his ear. Or some other thing. At the time this advice would have sounded to me as irrelevant as science fiction, not that I read that stuff either, and not that our relationship was destined to go anywhere fast other than downward, so reading those gal mags was never destined to be on my To Do List.

She gave me the salon phone number, which I kept for future reference, but I don't think I called. Instead, I did drop in on Jersey Boy. I was amicable, or tried to be. He assured me he was good for the money, half-ass apologized for inconveniencing her and me. Sure OK fine whatever. He gave me a personal check made out to me, asked me to wait a couple of days till his payroll check cleared.

Wait, a *check*? To the guy doing collection on your deadbeat ass? Did I puff out my chest and demand to see ID, his driver's license? Some kind of tough guy, me. And remember checks? Me, either.

I must have been suspicious, so the hell with waiting for some supposed payroll check to clear. I left his salon and immediately drove to his bank branch, determined to play it all out. Remember bank branches? Anyway, that's when the teller advised me that this checking account was closed. Therefore Jersey Boy and I were about to have a much bigger problem. What I mean is, the masculinity stakes seriously ratcheted up. He thought he could play me? I guess he was so desperate he had no choice. Either that, or he had no fear of me. I was going with the second possibility. My move now. I would soon find out if I was a poser, too, which was something I have intermittently half-suspected my entire life. And here's the whole reason why I bring up this story, and what I have been leading up to.

I must have spoken to my father about what was going on—and this is a development whose outlines I barely recall and cannot explain at all. It was not the kind of thing I did as a matter of course, seeking out his fatherly counsel and wisdom, so I cannot recollect the circumstances, or how or why I imagined it would have been constructive to talk to him, or if we had a conversation in person or on the phone. I do know for certain that he offered to be of assistance. *The guy's from Jersey, huh?* he might have wished to reconfirm. I must have told him about the bum check. *Give me the guy's number, I'll talk to him,* he must have said. I do recall I said his debt changed. It was now $220. It wasn't the money, it was the principle, *and* the money.

A day or so later, my father said the guy told him he had the cash and was ready to square up that night. It wouldn't have surprised me if he offered to ride along, but I probably would have said no thanks. A man's gotta do what a man's gotta do. And so do posers like me.

That night, as promised and on schedule, Jersey Boy and I had the briefest of conversations before he handed over the paper currency. He looked a bit shaken, or so I remember, and he said something like he didn't expect to get a phone call from somebody like that, which I took to mean that the old man had subtly intimated that it was in the guy's best interests to pay up, and that there would be unnamed consequences otherwise. And that's my clearest remembrance of my father's participation in—no, not really—the shakedown, because Jersey Boy was legitimately on the hook. My father must have been hardwired as to the right buttons to push, perfectly attuned to the right bells to ring. And no doubt a man who had been convicted of check forgery had at his disposal a few choice morsels of information on the subject of bank regulation.

Jersey Boy was full of himself, so he also remarked it was illegal for me to charge interest. I didn't know about that, but I reminded him, if that was true, so was drafting a fraudulent check. After that night, I never ran into the guy again, and my girlfriend was made financially whole, and I suppose she found another hairdresser. To this day, I do wonder if I gave her $200 or $220. I could have made a case either way. Any poser could.

More than anything, I realized if Jersey Boy hairdressers and questionable girlfriends with poor judgment were predictable, that was one thing I could never say about my old man. He still had game.

SHE DON'T LIE, SHE DON'T LIE,

SHE DON'T LIE

*S*cene: *Pretty people of a certain age dressed in white, flowing, imminently disposable clothes, ambling at sunset on the otherwise solitary California shoreline, hand in hand; rascally little bonfire sending up sparks; hey-there-now flutes canoodling in the come-hithery air.*

Smoky voiceover by a woman, oozing simultaneously power and submissiveness:

"Cocaine is not for everyone. Ask your doctor if you're unhealthy enough and if cocaine is right for you. If you experience the impulse to make middle-of-the-night booty calls, seek psychological help or, better yet, spiritual guidance. Do not use if you have high blood pressure, low blood pressure, or any blood pressure period. If after ingesting cocaine you have an erection lasting three hours, seek immediate medical attention—for your poor partner. Also notify the Guinness Book of

Records. After an eight ball, you'll be fortunate to have an erection lasting three minutes..."

∽

OLD JOKE. GUY DOES a line and somebody asks him why he does coke. Guy says, "To see God." "What does God tell you?" "God says don't do coke."

∽

"IT WAS LOVE AT first sight." That is the sentence that opens *Catch-22*. I loved that book and I loved this drug that also opened my eyes, and not in an optimal way. More accurately, my toothpick-propped-open coked-up peepers were unblinking as a hawk's when the dehooded raptor's talons grip the falconer's glove. As few of us were aware in the lost decade of the eighties and everybody knows now that love at first sight threatened to obliterate many a bank account, family, career, romance, and life. I could relate. Four for five; I hit for the cycle.

In those halcyon days, coke was widely considered a "recreational" drug. We should have seen through this marketing ploy. For "recreational" would have been an appropriate characterization if your idea of recreation was stabbing yourself in the neck, jabbering all night and not remembering a thing you or anybody else said, feeling like your skin was curling up like seared wallpaper in a red-tagged dwelling. Not right away, of course not. The first hit, a spoonful or a razor-chopped line, was like coming across a fabulous oasis in the middle of the endless desert. The fiftieth hit, later that night or more often the next morning, like trudging headfirst into a blinding sandstorm. I was stretched for rent money, grocery money, gas money, money money, and I was dealing. Intent to sell: trafficking in weight that could earn somebody many years in the slammer. Nonetheless, small time. Nobody called me El Jo Jo. Practically every day I committed a felony. Good days, a couple. I know, I know, I know. I was lucky.

⌒

COCAINE COCAINE COCAINE COCAINE COCAINE
COCAINE COCAINE COCAINE COCAINE COCAINE
COCAINE COCAINE COCAINE COCAINE COCAINE
COCAINE COCAINE COCAINE COCAINE COCAINE
COCAINE COCAINE COCAINE COCAINE COCAINE
COCAINE COCAINE COCAINE COCAINE COCAINE
COCAINE COCAINE COCAINE COCAINE COCAINE
COCAINE COCAINE COCAINE COCAINE COCAINE
COCAINE COCAINE COCAINE COCAINE COCAINE
COCAINE COCAINE COCAINE COCAINE COCAINE
COCAINE COCAINE COCAINE COCAINE COCAINE
COCAINE COCAINE COCAINE COCAINE COCAINE
COCAINE COCAINE COCAINE COCAINE COCAINE
COCAINE COCAINE COCAINE COCAINE COCAINE

COCAINE   COCAINE   COCAINE   COCAINE   COCAINE
COCAINE   COCAINE   COCAINE   COCAINE   COCAINE
COCAINE   COCAINE   COCAINE   COCAINE   COCAINE
COCAINE   COCAINE   COCAINE   COCAINE   COCAINE
COCAINE   COCAINE   COCAINE   COCAINE   COCAINE
COCAINE   COCAINE   COCAINE   COCAINE   COCAINE
COCAINE   COCAINE   COCAINE   COCAINE   COCAINE
COCAINE   COCAINE   COCAINE   COCAINE   COCAINE

❧

MY BROTHER INTRODUCED ME to coke, though that was not his drug of choice. We were opposites in school and in most aspects of everyday style and substance, including when it came to drugs. *His* depressant, *my* stimulant.

In *The Noonday Demon*, Solomon writes about depression and the linkages with addiction and drugs: "Depression and substance abuse form a cycle. People who are depressed abuse substances in a bid to free themselves of their depression. People who abuse substances disrupt their lives to the point that they become depressed by the damage." "Depressants such as…heroin relieve anxiety and aggravate depression; stimulants such as cocaine relieve depression and aggravate anxiety." Bookends, my brother and I.

Solomon continues: "Opiates…are extremely dangerous in part because of how they are consumed; and they are depressants, which means that they do not do great things for depression. On the other hand, they don't lead to the kind of desperate crash that cocaine will bring about… Opiates blot out time, so that you cannot remember where your thoughts come from, cannot tell whether they are new or old, cannot get them to interact with one another. The world closes in around you… It is the experience of perfect not-wanting… Opiates are classed as depressants, but their effect is not simple suppression of feelings; it is a species of joy that comes of having your feelings suppressed. On opiates, you can give anxious depression the slip." Whereas on cocaine, "I get to the point of being unable to string together a sentence again and I don't care if I never string together a sentence again. I realize that the solutions to everything are simple and straightforward. Being high on cocaine breaks up your memory enough so that the past can't haunt the future. The chemical happiness of a good hit of cocaine feels completely uncircumstantial… [I]f I could freeze life in that second, I would do so and stay there forever."

John and I were both divided and connected by our depression and addiction. We were also divided and connected through our dad's depression and his compulsive gambling. Research referenced by Solomon shows that addiction pathways (such as for compulsive gambling) are in the brain "and that the object of the compulsion is not really significant…; addiction to behaviors does not differ significantly from addiction to substances. It is the helpless need to keep repeating something damaging that drives dependence, rather than the physiological response to the thing repeated."

Three peas in a fuckin' pod.

～

"SHE DON'T LIE, SHE don't lie, she don't lie," sang Eric Clapton, "cocaine," though it was transparent she sort of did, and proceeds to riff out. The Grateful Dead was flying high back then, too: "Drivin' that train, high on cocaine..." But in my mind no band compared to the Eagles when it came to coke times.

That contention might reveal more about me and my banal middlebrow sensibilities than it does about the granulated, empowdery culture at large. Guilty as charged. Don't suppose saying that Hall & Oates was a strong backup in my mind for that distinction will garner me any more cred on the street. Didn't think so (though everybody says the eighties are back now). Maybe I could attribute my middlebrow sensibilities to my devotion to a definitively middlebrow stimulant. Was that an era when there was always playing on the car cassette player or in the dive bar some song by the Eagles? It seemed that way. Maybe they weren't the Temptations or Marvin Gaye or Otis Redding or Springsteen or the Allman Brothers or the Stones or Zeppelin, but with their brand of bluegrass slash country slash rock slash inhalable or injectable or stimulized LA, they captured the skittery jittery juiced-up mood—if not *the*, then *my* mood. In and of itself, *that* says everything about the drug: omniscience and absolute certitude on call. *On a dark, desert highway… Welcome to the Hotel California… You can't hide your lyin' eyes… Witchy woman, see how high she flies… Victim of love… Lines on the mirror, lines on her face… Take it to the limit… Life in the fast lane… Try and love again… Freeways, cars, and trucks… Freedom, that's just some people talkin'… Look at us, baby, up all night… You got your demons, you got desires, I got a few of my own… I am already gone …*

Chances are, you had to be there. But while bubbling and bobbing in that chemical brew maybe nobody was really there. There *was* somebody there who got my earnest attention when she said that whenever she heard the Eagles, she thought about me, and she made plain that she meant that in a very promising way, so imagine where that was going, beyond earnestly, for a minute.

All in all, this was a horrible time of shag carpets and shag haircuts, when I was roughly the same age as my father when he got into all of his trouble. Feeling powerless before the drug, sometimes I looked for a way out and I'd go to Mass by myself, Newman Hall at UC Berkeley. It didn't really work. Of course, as I settled into the pew, I was high.

It takes a certain sort of out-of-mindset to do that next line knowing that you have no choice but to do that next line and it's a very bad idea, that you're going to regret it, that you are going to hate yourself, and that you have a choice but are too weak to resist. What are you chasing, what are you fleeing? Is it the same thing? Self-loathing: is it the byproduct or is it the purpose? Sure, anybody can cite the brain research that cuts a path through the numbness to the hot nerve of absurdity. You know what the drug did to the lab rats who gave up water, sex, food, everything, for a taste. Blessed lab rats. At least they died. A drug that creates the need for itself: it expertly, insidiously, chemically mimics whatever we hold precious in our lives. I'm talking to myself. That's what the drug does to you. It's a one-way, endless loop. Another name for addiction.

Never enough. Never high enough. Never enough product at hand. Never enough. Bindles and vials everywhere. Scales and baggies in the closet. Hundreds, and then thousands in my pocket, sales and buys conducted with a reliable clientele. Late at night I'd count out the cash and pore over ads for cars, deciding which BMW I would buy. Never did buy one of those. Usually profits went up my nose. What's the business model again? A depressing, sleepless cycle.

My father called gambling his "vice." Was coke my vice? That idea also fits to a T. This is a mysterious idiom, possibly historically related to T-shirt, in which case, the T-shirt here would be made of horse hair. Then again, being obsessive-compulsive as I am, I could also view my addiction in terms of that anxiety disorder, too. For cocaine is a drug tailor-made for the OCD set. So that also fits to a T. Was coke my gateway to a life of crime? On some level, it could have been, but wasn't. Just so you know, nothing really fits to a T with regard to coke. It was a terrible time, I am guilty, I am a sick man.

I thought I heard wake-up calls from time to time. Meaning every night. Time to stop, this is killing you. This is called wasting your life. I pressed the snooze alarm, not that snoozing was an option.

⤳

MY FATHER NEVER OFFERED much in the way of fatherly advice, but I recall a few *bons mots* along lines like these, repeated over the years:

Don't take no shit from nobody.

Don't count your money in front of no windows.

Don't get clipped.

Don't cry.

Don't bet with a bookmaker. (Seriously? Seriously.)

Mostly don'ts.

What are some of the memorable lessons I acquired from my father?

How to throw a baseball. (Efforts resulting in mixed if not negligible results.)

How to ride a bike.

How to eat spaghetti. (Forget the stupid spoon and don't talk while you're eating, you could choke.)

How to file a fraudulent insurance claim. (Which I did without an ounce of moral compunction once, and possibly twice, when

268 ～ J O S E P H   D I   P R I S C O

flat broke, in my early twenties. The old post-rear-ender whiplash boondoggle; chiropractors, ambulance-chasing lawyers, everybody knows about this.)

How to drive. (He was a good driver and he tried.)

How to check the oil level in the car and the tire pressure.

How to maintain a poker face, and how to speak in plausibly deniable English formulations.

How to make a vodka gimlet. This qualified as useless information; bad drink.

How to drive after the vodka gimlets, or when sleepy. (Open all the windows, obviously.)

How to use masking and duct tape. (That is, on about every broken or frayed thing.)

How to tie a tie and polish shoes.

How to deal with my mother when she was pissed. (I would enjoy innumerable opportunities to practice this simple strategy, in which I almost emulated his example. For him, it meant going to the track. Since I didn't go to the track, I took off.)

Most valuable lesson he taught: I needed to be a better father. Not that he put it that way. You see, one exception to the rule of all his don'ts I learned the time I dropped off my son with him and my mother—Mario must have been five or six. I think I was coming down from the night before, and I had enough sense to have my boy, who loved them, hang with them. Their relationship with him was maybe the high point of their family life. I was, and am, grateful.

He wanted to say something he regarded as important, I could tell: one, by the fact that he wanted my attention, and two, by the fact that he was talking. He said:

"They grow up fast."

I was shaken. He was right. I wouldn't lose my time with my boy as a child. I would get myself together. He was right. And I heard an echo of some other voice of understanding, and more than that, of loss. I heard him regretting the years he had lost with his own boys, who grew up fast, and without him.

~

YET I DOUBT I instantly turned over a new leaf. But then I heard another sort of radical wake-up call. My supplier abruptly went out of business, which signaled to me that this was the time I myself should take the opportunity to hang up the CLOSED shingle.

I had had a good run with Mickey ever since we got to know each other as incompetent waiters at an Italian restaurant and later as members of the blackjack team in Reno, Tahoe, and Vegas. He was a brilliantly street-smart guy with a soft heart but had no crisis of conscience busting up somebody he didn't like or who disrespected him, out here in the world or in San Quentin, where he did a serious bit for dealing major weight of what he called H. You'd be nuts to pick

270 ~ JOSEPH DI PRISCO

a fight with him or flirt with his girlfriend. But what if his girlfriend comes on to you when he passed out drunk that time and you took her home? I am glad he never found out about that, and all men are mad dogs, in case any elves out there remain in the dark. He drove a beautiful, blue Corvette, and we would go to bars and he would hold forth on one subject or another—family, fatherhood, friendship, money, romance. "Don't think," he would opine, in a typical aside, "just 'cause the bitch fucks you on the first night you're anything special." I struggled to agree, but I wasn't as smart as he was, and his track record with women was dicey, to say the least. So we had a little bit in common.

He didn't leave the business by choice, and I would very much miss him. That's because Mickey was also my good friend, and that's also because one night, while he was tweaking on crack, he was stabbed to death.

It took me a long time to clean up, but maybe addiction is ultimately not in my DNA. Maybe survival is, maybe fear, maybe cowardice. I needed another line of work. Out of nowhere, I got a teaching job and never did another line. It took me a long time to realize how fortunate I had been. How come it didn't feel that way?

Poets have famously loved their drugs, doors of perception, visions of Kubla Khan a stately pleasure dome decreed, radically changing the sight lines, that sort of thing. Poets are by nature inclined to look for infinite vistas, views from the precipice of eternity. Hey, news flash. Spiritual masters all say such vistas, such views are omnipresent and accessible, if you're looking in the right way. So I hear. But what drugs did for me was the opposite. They made me realize the absolute finitude of time. Time I was expending on nothing ultimately worth knowing or having. I'm not judging. Well, I am, but I'm judging myself. What's more, they made me realize the finitude of me. Because for me, the drug high amounted to the prospect of an imminent toe tag. Once upon a time, not that I can clock it, not at all, I used to have an infinite number of nights left to live. And then, one night, cocaine was all over for me. Like a death. But a strange death, one from which I could get up and walk away from, like a minor-league Lazarus, so I did.

New York State Appellate Division

RECORDS AND BRIEFS

Q. Day of the alleged occurrence?

A. It was cold weather.

Q. No, I know it was cold, it was February?

A. You asked me.

Q. Was it raining, or snowing?

A. No.

Q. Rained at all, that day?

A. I don't know if it rained. I know it was cold.

Q. Don't remember if it was raining or not?

A. Pardon me?

Q. Snowing?

A. Cold, not raining.

Q. Not raining, wasn't snowing?

A. I was standing outside when it happened.

Q. Was not raining or snowing?

A. That's right.

Q. Was it raining or snowing when you met in the diner, that was an hour before?

A. Not that I remember.

Q. Try to remember?

A. I came by subway.

Q. I know you got out on the street, didn't you?

A. That's right.

Q. Was it raining at 4 o'clock, snowing at 4 o'clock, clear at 4 o'clock?

A. We got into the car.

Caza of Brooklyn with Radio.

WHAT LARKS

After my high-rolling blackjack career bounced into the ravine of busted, I worked as a general manager of Italian restaurants and later as a wine consultant. The so-called hospitality industry would not ultimately be for me, and I was no oenological genius like Robert Parker, all of which must be apparent by now. Nobody else ever asked me where I saw myself in five years, and neither did I, so don't get any ideas, wise guy.

Finally I accepted reality. I was tap city. Well, I remember having exactly thrity-five dollars in the checking account, the proud possessor of a maxed-out credit card, and gradually inured to the daily hectoring of collection agencies. I had a child to support. It's the worst, most hopeless feeling. This also feels a little like death. Only expiration with ongoing consciousness and guilt and unpaid bills piling up.

My graduate fellowship at Berkeley had run out long ago, and academic job prospects looked bleaker and bleaker by the day for somebody like me. I interviewed at colleges here and there, but insofar as transplanting thousands of miles away constituted a nonstarter (as I could not tolerate living so far away from my son), my professorial ambitions were DOA.

Then in the fall of 1986 a renowned little independent high school in San Francisco hired me. In absolute terms, a professional comedown, perhaps, but I was grateful and set aside my pride. I went cold turkey: no drugs, no alcohol. I would come to realize quickly that my students were sophisticated and hilarious, complicated and joyous, demanding and generous, the quality of their thinking and writing rivaling the University of California undergraduates I had taught. Was adolescence my natural habitat? It might have been, because three years into my tenure the seniors elected me to give their commencement speech, representing the faculty—the first of two occasions I would be chosen to speak at the school graduation. In June 1989, Tiananmen Square and the political crackdown in China were on everybody's mind that gray overcast morning in Julius Kahn Park. As I look over the remarks I made, I see things I would nowadays frame somewhat differently, but it's folly to rewrite the past. I found myself saying things that mattered to me, about teaching and learning and growing up. The words feel dated here and there—crushing on Kathleen Turner and all—but that's also all right, so am I.

My students turned me around, bestowed me with purpose and clarity, and my work gave me some essential stability. Despite their gift to me, that graduation speech day, I was a nervous wreck. You know, speaking in public is very different from teaching a class. A class is intimate, anything but public; I always felt at home in a classroom, as a student or instructor. In 1989, I was as yet unaccustomed to presenting before large groups. Also on my mind was that my son, due to enter this high school in the fall on financial aid, without which he could not have attended, had a championship Little League baseball game that day. I was crestfallen to miss it. When I returned home I discovered that he had pitched a no-hitter—and took the loss. Doesn't that say it all about growing up? Also that day, something else of great significance happened to me. I met the woman who would before long become my wife. She was attending the ceremonies because her goddaughter was graduating. Who can plan for anything?

This is what I said, over twenty-five years ago, on that cloudy San Francisco morning:

∽

LET ME BEGIN WITH *a confession. No need to scramble, it's not going to be* that *kind of confession.*

Recently I have sensed burgeoning within me, like the mysterious monster that plays pop-goes-the-weasel in the Alien *movies, a dark fantasy. The fantasy has nothing to do with time travel, or with pitching in the World Series, or with climbing in the Himalayas, or with doing lunch in Florence with Kathleen Turner—intriguing as all these fantasies may indeed be—especially that one about lunch.*

Please let me explain. I want to explain because I feel profoundly honored, touched, and flattered to be invited by you to speak today. And as I struggled with what I wanted to say, I came to understand what lay at the bottom of this wish. It's the wish to say something—corny and clichéd as it sounds—something that will change your lives.

That's the confession part. What an incredible, what an arrogant wish it must seem: the wish to change somebody's life. But you know, changing somebody's life is the most ordinary objective in the world. It's the implicit goal in every single class; it's the exhortation written in invisible ink at the top of each and every lesson plan. If teachers really didn't feel on some level that they wanted to change somebody's life, they would be filling out applications to law school, making movies, driving racecars, doing ad campaigns for a cute dog and his favorite beer. Oh, sure, obviously torts, and shows, and fast cars, and slogans change people's lives (in some cases much more quickly than others, and in many cases for the better), but I believe what goes on in the classroom is a little bit different.

I have been your English teacher, that is, someone who taught you some books. But I hope you won't misunderstand when I say that I am simply an English teacher. When I say that I don't believe I am being

278   JOSEPH DI PRISCO

modest or self-effacing. Why start now?—you're too polite to ask, thank you. So let's talk about what you learned when you learned how to read literature.

What exactly happened to you when you read a great novel? What did you have when you finished a story? What could you keep, what could you use? And knowing stories, what is it that you know? Yourselves? The world? Yourselves in the world? The world in yourselves? Do you find that, along with me, you are getting a headache right now, too?

Hypothetically, there should be nothing easier to talk about. In the continental United States, this year alone, according to some very reliable statistics, which I have made up, 64 million class hours were devoted to the treatment of some 6,000 novels, 17 million hours devoted to some 365,000 poems (not counting "Stopping by Woods on a Snowy Evening" by Robert Frost). And somewhere, every waking and sleeping moment of the school day, an average of 4.23 students accidentally, tragically land on "But soft! What light through yonder window breaks?"—a line from Romeo and Juliet, the Shakespeare play based on the far superior Franco Zeferelli movie. All this makes you think that somebody must know what's going on, reading books, assigning papers, doesn't it?

Here's a parable. The reason I call it a parable is that I have no idea what it means, and because if I call it a parable, perhaps nobody will summon the cold nerve to ask for an explanation. Verily, I say unto you that it came to pass once in the land of Pacific Heights that a student of *mine was accosted by one pilgrim named Louis Knight, my colleague, and asked, "If you could throw out one play by Shakespeare, what would it be?" Disgusted and courageous, she replied, "Hamlet." "OK," he kept after her (because he is Louis Knight, ladies and gentlemen). "If you could keep only one play by Shakespeare, what would it be?" She hesitated, but she was honest: "Hamlet," she said. What is going on here?*

It is well-known to educators and to everyone else that there are good books and bad books, profound books and boring books, inspiring books and deflating books. Of course, one person's King Lear *is another's* Nurse Cathy's Revenge. *And what one person thinks is essential reading, a great book, is nothing more than a dreary "classic" to somebody else. (If I had the time today, I could show the difference, but that will have to wait.) And if we took a survey of all the required reading that all your teachers think you should have completed by the time you graduate, you would be many years away from your commencement. Now, it is also well-known to sociologists, afternoon TV talk show hosts, bonehead evangelists, Supreme Court justices, and English teachers that literature bears some relation to what we too confidently refer to as "real life." But what is that relation?*

Furthermore, what does it mean to read literature in a world ravaged by the lethal mystery of AIDS, a world of Bangladeshes and Ethiopias, a world flirting with ecological disaster, a world in which students very much like you are massacred in the pursuit of democracy

280 ~ JOSEPH DI PRISCO

in China? Could there be anything more precious, more beside the point, more trivial than losing ourselves in a book?

And make no mistake about it, the twentieth century will be remembered as the age of totalitarianism. Isn't it remarkable that every tyrant must burn books, must bomb schools, must murder writers and teachers and students? This point has been driven home this last week by the deplorable events in Beijing, and it was driven home to me in my travels last year to Cambodia, where I visited Tuol Sleng, the Belsen of the Khmer Rouge. Here is where they extracted false written confessions from their prisoners, and their prisoners included every student, teacher, and writer they could get their hands on. Here you can see in place the preferred instruments of torture, blood still stains the floors. If you listen too hard you make yourself believe you can hear the echoing voices of these victims, inextinguishable including in death. Tuol Sleng, it is spooky and essential to realize, was once upon a time a school.

The Pol Pots, the Chairman Maos, the Joseph Stalins, the Pinochets, do not think literature is trivial, but it isn't my intention to grant them any sort of credit. Far from it. It's just that suppressed people understand all too well the moral truth and the power of the imagination, which we in a free society may, at our cost, take for granted. Imagination is the enemy of authority and of brutality; it is the nemesis of injustice; it is the dream of freedom. And literature, writing it, reading it, discussing it, teaching it, constitutes an adversarial, subversive, critical act. Reading books is dangerous, because it encourages us to call into question the absolute certitude of power.

Beyond that, reading books brings with it kinds of responsibilities, and these are the kinds of responsibilities that help us understand we are human beings; they make us realize we are citizens in a democracy, residents of the planet Earth, creatures of history as well as creators of history.

Though it would be foolish to say that books constitute the whole of education, and though it would be cowardly to live in an ivory tower full of fabulations and fictions, action in the world is wiser action when fired by the imagination. That's why I like so much what a student said in summary comment about a class: "I like that class," she said, "because we talked about things I usually keep in the back of my mind." For something amazing happens in the middle of a discussion of a great piece of writing. We sense that something matters beyond ourselves, that we need to take a stand. Sometimes it is very hard to know what this stand is, or means, and yet it is important to take. Something about reading this book means something crucial about living our lives. We find ourselves in the middle of a secret, and the secret is that we are all alive. We find ourselves in the middle of a surprise, and the surprise is that we have been here all along. The surprise is that we are not alone in our suffering or in our dreams.

In this regard, I wouldn't want to leave you today without putting in a good word for unhappiness. I'm not talking about depression, which is a terrible clinical condition, or about sadness, which is an altogether reasonable response to mortality, but about unhappiness. There's a lot to be said for good will, raucous and inappropriate humor, uplifted spirits, and you graduating seniors brought that mood all the time into the classroom. (And when friends ask me what I like about teaching at University High School, one of the things I say is that I can't remember a day when I didn't laugh, really laugh, about something that happened in school.) But anyway, literature is more than the pleasant expression of "profound sentiments."

So a perennially happy student is one ... who didn't get the reading done. For literature is often written in despair and in rage, by the dispossessed and the marginalized. And education, I believe, should cultivate discontent, discontent with the world as it is, and it should nurture deep unease, unease with the lives we receive. A good student is, by definition, in some way inconsolable.

That's where imagination storms in: to console the inconsolable. It enables us to ask better questions. Instead of: What's in it for me? What can I get away with? Who cares? Am I my brother's keeper? We ask: What makes someone a human being? What do we do now with this time we have together? What do we do now, faced with a bad king, a terrible and tragic war, sickness unto death, a universe racing to entropy? How do we confront evil? How do we pursue the good? Always a more beautiful answer, said the wiseguy poet e.e. cummings, to a more beautiful question. Always a more beautiful answer to a more beautiful question.

In Tim O'Brien's great novel about the war in Vietnam, Going After Cacciato, *the protagonist, Paul Berlin, imagines peace in the form of a stupid G.I., a soldier so stupid he believes he can leave the war, and who walks, it seems, all the way to Paris. Sarkin Aung Wan, the imaginary Vietnamese woman whom Paul Berlin loves, tells him: "You have come far… You have taken many risks. You have been brave beyond your wildest expectations. And now it is time for a final act of courage. I urge you: March proudly into your own dream." March proudly into your own dream. The world tells you to straighten up and fly right, to face reality. The imagination says, March proudly into your own dream. "In dreams," said the great Irish political poet William Butler Yeats, "in dreams begin responsibilities."*

Now that I have tried to show you all that I think literature does, I am going to leave you with something that may seem to undercut my argument. It doesn't, however. Most of you are familiar with the wonderful novel by Charles Dickens, Great Expectations. *Great expectations are rightfully on your mind today. And I want you to recall that novel for one minute. It is a story of education and disillusionment, love and money. Pip, the poor orphan, gets a glimpse of privilege and the upper class through something like awful good luck. Pip learns what really matters. One of his best teachers turns out to be the nearly illiterate, noble Joe Gargery, the poor honest man who raised him.*

Joe never fails to remember the larks, the good times they shared. What larks, *they continually remind themselves. Of course, Pip breaks Joe's heart, and of course—this is Dickens—Joe forgives him. As it is time to say goodbye to you, then, I take solace in some exchanges between Pip and Joe, the blacksmith.*

"Pip, dear old chap, life is made of ever so many partings welded together, as I may say, and one man's a blacksmith, and one's a whitesmith, and one's a coppersmith. Divisions among such must come, and must be met as they come." And so it is with you graduates today. Your parents and your teachers must meet this division, must articulate this goodbye.

Much later on, when Pip and Joe separate again, Pip says, "It has been a memorable time for me, Joe... We have had a time together, Joe, that I can never forget. There were days once, I know, that I did for a while forget, but I shall never forget these."

"Pip," said Joe, appearing a little hurried and troubled, "there has been larks. And...what has been betwixt us—have been."

What larks.

What larks.

ONE HAPPY BIRTHDAY

Y ou chew the aspirin because it works faster. Seconds count when it comes to addressing the blockages to your heart. Amazing, how much knowledge you can aquire flat on a gurney, looking up toward the ceiling tiles if not heaven. Then the nitroglycerin tab was administered sublingually, and my head throbbed, right on schedule, a fair price to pay for desired vasodilation. Nitroglycerin has a bitter taste, but I was rolling around on my tongue *sublingually*, a sweet word. I was also thinking this was shaping up to be a strange birthday. I was hoping it wouldn't be my last.

When I appeared at my doctor's reception desk a few moments before, I was woozy, and I complained about a powerful pressure in my chest like I had never felt. The other details now blur. I was led to a seat and somebody called 911. Every twenty-five seconds somebody in America is having a coronary event. So far none of these Americans had been me.

The fire department arrived.

"What hospital do you prefer?"

I must have been disoriented because I said, "Someplace in Rome."

"Good idea," the fireman said. "I've never been."

Come on, Rome may be my favorite city on earth, but I should have opted for exactly where I was, the Bay Area, Northern California. They did an EKG. There was reason. It was as if a python had wrapped itself around my chest; I was sweating and lightheaded. My arm tingled. My throat hurt. Blood pressure was through the roof.

"Do you have family?"

I scanned my memory bank for Zorba the Greek's reply to that very question, "Wife, children, the full catastrophe," but I came up blank.

"Is there somebody we should call?"

In the back of my mind, I was reasoning: if my wife or son showed up it would prove I was in big trouble. If they didn't, maybe this wasn't happening.

Three years earlier, the celebration of my birthday with a zero in the number took the form of a fake prom. It was held in a school gym, thematically decorated. One hundred fifty friends were attired as for their own big high school night. A portrait photographer immortalized images against a cheesy retro backdrop. The fabulous R&B band hired for the occasion let me sing lead for The Temptations' "Ain't Too Proud to Beg" and Sam Cooke's "You Send Me." My tux-wearing son, the consummate MC and roaster, got the laugh when he suggested it was past time for me to buy wine futures. Perfect night. Perfection was not my aspiration now. My current, pressing goal was tomorrow.

Once in the ER, a flurry of activity. Behind the drawn curtain I was attended to by what appeared to be a score of eerily professional and ethereally kind men and women, a diversity of age and race and ethnicity, a snapshot of California. More EKGs, a chest X-ray, two more nitroglycerin tabs, blood draws. The oxygen refreshed. The monitors beeped and chuffed, buzzed and hummed.

"What day is it?"

"Who is the president?"

"What is your name?"

"Where do you live?"

"What is the year?"

"What is your name?

"What is the year?"

The attending, who looked young enough to have once been a student of mine, gently but firmly broke the news. My ticket had been punched for the night. I was going to be admitted. The first furious round of blood test results and EKGs were encouraging, but we had a ways to go. I balked at the prospect of a hospital stay. "It's my birthday," I said. Patti and I had dinner reservations. The doc glanced at my hospital wristband identification to verify. "It *is* your birthday." He returned two minutes later bearing a chocolate cupcake with swirled blue icing, a tongue depressor serving as a candle. "Happy birthday."

On birthdays I usually try and summarily fail to write a poem. My attempts invariably lead to meaning-of-life dime store philosophy, which is the death knell of poetry. I long ago resigned myself. Never would I compose my version of Dylan Thomas's great "Poem in October": "It was my thirtieth year to heaven…"

The chest pressure by now had alleviated. Calm settled over me, the wait for resolution commenced. Alone inside my darkened, curtained-off space I felt the hours slowly pass, like boats approaching the horizon. Having nothing to do, I struggled to solve mentally a problem afflicting a new book I was working on. I got nowhere. I hoped the point would not become moot. I took a peek at what was downloaded onto my phone, read a mystery written in grade school Italian, then tried some Montaigne, my favorite, but nothing was filtering through.

Only then did I call my wife. She was distressed. I told her not to worry. Note to self: when has that move ever worked? She wanted to come to the hospital. Let's wait, I insisted, irrationally confident I would be discharged soon. She reluctantly complied. Was denial a virus going around today?

I may have dozed. A wonderful nurse appeared. I don't believe I hallucinated her. In four hours they would draw more blood. They were on the trail of an enzyme called troponin. It is a reliable marker of a cardiac event, and they needed a retest. She looked optimistic. The ER may be a strange location to promote social intimacy, but it could be the opposite. She wanted to know if I was Italian. She once had an Italian boyfriend, she confided. She said every woman needed at least one Italian bad boy boyfriend. I couldn't validate that point, but this did not prevent her from throwing out some idiomatic expressions, including "Ti voglio bene," the charmingly indirect Italian way of saying "I love you." She wasn't addressing me, but it was nice to hear the sentiment anyway.

Afterward I couldn't help but listen to the disembodied voices bouncing off the walls. The abject moaning, as of a suffering animal, from a far-off corner. The demented but eloquent articulations of an elderly woman one bed over, invisible behind the curtain. The rich baritone of docs examining one patient after another. "Where did you get these bruises?" "How many times did you fall?" "Do you remember if you ate today?" "Take a deep breath."

As lightning bolts go, here's one I should have seen coming. Where else would I prefer to be on my birthday if not here? It was good to be reminded, as if I needed to be, how brief life is, how tenuous the hold we have on our loved ones. The makings of a poem? No, at least not for me. And the dime store philosophy seemed anything but.

My doctor eventually informed me test results had all gone my way. "It's probably a negligible risk being discharged, but you need to see the cardiologist right away, do a treadmill test ASAP. Happy birthday."

So this was a fake heart attack?

"It's a good thing you came in," said the doctor.

I dressed and got into my car.

Walking into my home after spending eight hours in the ER, I could see I may have made a bad mistake not encouraging Patti to come to the hospital. I could tell she was very distraught. "Some kind of birthday," she said. We plied free a few rogue EKG tabs clinging to my chest, my legs. "I'm glad you're here," she said. "It's not the same without you."

No one had ever said such a thing to me before. I found the woman I was always looking for.

New York State Appellate Division

RECORDS AND BRIEFS

Q. And what else did he tell you?

A. He told me they scored for two thousand dollars.

Q. Two thousand dollars!

A. Yes.

Q. Now, did you receive any money of this?

A. Yes, I received about two hundred dollars on the first payment.

Q. And was there a second payment?

A. Yes, sir.

Q. Now, and of that second payment, how much did you receive?

A. Fifty dollars.

Q. Fifty dollars. Did Celentano ever lend you money?

A. Yes, sir, two instances. He sent me seventy-five dollars, once up in Lake George, and he advanced me about another fifty dollars.

Q. And what was the other fifty dollars for?

A. Well, to—I had—I was trying to get a line on a stickup, and I had to be with these people drinking, and things like that.

The Truth, the Whole Truth,
and Something Like the Truth

For most of my college years I was in thrall to Not-Naomi. But I mean that in a good way. She easily deserves the less-than-coveted All-time First Girlfriend Prize. I could go on at exhaustive length to convince you how she qualifies, but this is the clincher for me: we're still friends. At an early stage of our liaison, she passed along what her uncannily perceptive, professorial mother said about what you must know by now is a favorite subject of mine: me. Her mom made the observation that Joe obviously raised himself. When people raise themselves, she added, they often have a void they spend their whole lives trying to fill. Her brilliant, incandescently literate daughter had witnessed that chaotic project firsthand for herself. Who knows? Maybe Mom was not so subtly suggesting to her child that she ought to run for the hills.

Whaddayou, Not-Naomi's mom, writin' a book?

294   JOSEPH DI PRISCO

I took the point. Did I have a choice? I had taken it before, and since then I have never stopped taking it and I expect I always will. For a long while I had been intellectually infatuated with the concept of the void; the whole madcap gang of once-upon-a-time fashionable existentialists and nihilists and relativists and anarchists spoke to me in a language I thought I could access. Saint John of the Cross's "dark night of the soul" probably did not amount to the void, but the distinction was as a practical matter missed by me. And Camus and Nietzsche and Heidegger and Kafka and Beckett? Common sense.

I think most of us have some sense of the void's existence. Many of us have been at least accidental tourists or unenthusiastic visitors passing through, some of us are resident aliens, a few of us connoisseurs or citizens, reluctant or otherwise.

So yes, indeed, the void. Dot dot dot.

My brother John attempted to fill the void in his own fashion, mainlining smack and committing crimes required to sustain his habit, struggling to survive his years in prison and on the street. He was a wounded soul. But in other ways and at other times, he also filled it with his abiding friendships and loyalties, and the spillage of an overflowing big heart. One way he was never able to fill that void was with the love of his parents: either the love they had for him, or his for them. Whatever they offered him in the name of parental love wasn't adequate. I can hold them accountable, and I often have, but that doesn't seem justified, quite. Drug addiction is merciless. Sooner or later, it crushes everybody in its purview, if given a chance. I do know for sure that the void swallowed John up.

I could say something similar about my dad. He tried to fill his void with gambling, with the thrill of the action, with the excitement of his criminality, with taking untenable risks. Later he attempted something comparable with his dedicated union work. I do think he valued, in some primitive sense, his family, but we weren't up to the task. I am confident when I say that in his mind we all let him down. His marriage made him miserable, but it was the best he could do.

I'd like to put in a few paltry semi-good words for the void.

As for me, well, the void got the best of me sometimes, I cannot deny or dispute it. There are those nights when emptiness can seem almost beautiful and bracing. Other nights, not so much. What's more, I don't know that people like me can ever perfectly or permanently fill the void. The emptiness and the darkness have their allure, which is not the word, for a depressed person. It certainly had such sway over me. I have spent the greater part of my life filling that emptiness with whatever I could, hoping for something to stick. In the past, with manic romantic entanglements or with drugs. More productively and sanely, and more recently, with my own work, reading and writing and teaching. A class that goes well, working with a student who is touched by self-understanding, those are fulfilling experiences. And finding the right words, shaping a poem or a novel, those are fine, lasting things. Not to mention marriage to a loving mate—who has proven to be a lifesaver. And a connection with a loving son, and his family, including grandkids. And friendships that I cannot imagine being without.

What about my spiritual life, if such a hallowed term could be applied to my endless search and riddling doubt? Good question, and fair. That's harder to talk about. And potentially an invitation to utter cringeworthy admissions. For one thing, I am disgusted by the endemic religious posturing in American culture, which is most glaringly in evidence on the part of politicians seeking votes by piously stipulating Jesus is Lord. If you're like me, when you hear these clowns, don't you want to punch them in their hypocritical noses? On this score, I have a dream. My dream is one day to throw in with a presidential candidate who replies, when interrogated about his or her religious convictions, "None of your business." A candidate reminiscent of the acerbic basketball coach genius Greg Popovich. Either somebody like that or an atheist who can understand the Constitution of this secular nation. For all the culturally dated piety about "one nation under God," the game-changing experiment that is the United States of America is founded not only upon the separation of church and state (or is it church and *taste*?) but equality, and it's built upon the rock of religious tolerance, specifically tolerance for un- and non- and disbelief. Amen.

Since I have referenced throughout how my little boy's faith mattered so much to me—should I say saved me?—I feel an obligation to follow up here with an account of my adult take. Here goes, such as it is. My Catholicism works for me, a fair amount of the time. When I was a tyke clutching at straws, that was one thing. Now, it's decidedly different, though the continuum between then and now is real. I'm no proselytizer, but I think Pope Francis might be up to something pretty good. We'll see what is his whole plan, though he has made a terrific start on climate change and on his full-throated emphasis upon serving the poor. (With your blessing, Your Holiness, were I you and I'm obviously not, I would push the Church to get over itself immediately on contraception, on gay marriage, on female clergy, and on priestly celibacy. As you said, "Who am I to judge?" Just saying, with respect, and thank you.)

I recognize that some worthy Catholics may not regard my Catholicism as Catholicism at all. I almost wish I possessed their self-gratulatory assurance. To them I would say, with all the charity I can muster, fuck the fuck off, please, and take your Jansenistic baggage with you as you deplane. (Jansenism is the namesake heresy attributed to the seventeenth century ultimate wet blanket of a Bishop Jansen who held no party spellbound hyperventilating the message that grace is available to the select few, the kind of guy who hides the IPA away from the mitts of nothing nobodies.) And as for those who find allegiance to any type of Catholicism intellectually indefensible if not comically naïve, I am comforted that these critics have figured out their lives. Yes, the pedophilia scandal is no mere blip on the screen. The all-too-human political institution of the Catholic Church crushed children, ruined families, failed itself. It will take generations to recover, if it ever does. I am able to make the skeptics' case—I have in fact made their case—but it doesn't ultimately hold water for me. I almost wish I had command of their depthless certainty.

Beyond that, I have not much more to add. In general, I feel I have a long way to go before understanding what this all means, but here's what I do know, and it's the only leg I have to stand on. The rituals have power for me. The days, the moments, when I feel the presence of something sacred in my life make the mystery and confusion and yes, the void, for a minute anyway, tolerable.

"The road of excess," wrote William Blake, "leads to the palace of wisdom."

Tell me about it.

No, really, somebody please tell me about it.

Blake also wrote in the same poem, "The Marriage of Heaven and Hell," "You never know what is enough unless you know what is more than enough."

⌒

IN SOME SENSE, A work of memory aspires to escape the past in order to illuminate or somehow inform, if not quite authenticate, the present. At least the author of such a work aspires as much. A memoir aspires to inhabit history so as to wrest meaning not merely from the past but to discover it in the present. But what does the present mean? To what extent is it knowable? The tricky part is that the one way to begin to understand where one has been before is to see where one is now. Only that *now* is a treacherously slippery place upon which to gain footing. Sometimes it's an oil slick, and you take a messy, grease-monkey tumble. Sometimes it's a frozen pond, which is melting beneath you in the springtime. Maybe you keep skating, oscillating between the past and the prospect of the future, all to the end of understanding the now. That's why the facts and the recollections, however conceptualized, are in service of a narrative, which is an account, a version, a selection, a myth. But perhaps curiously, there's a way in which crafting a fiction—a novel, a story, a poem—makes it less of a trial to tell the truth, because it's all made up. To some extent the experience of one's so-called real life informs an author's fiction— as how could it, to some significant degree, not? Memoir is not for the faint of heart, and neither is ordinary existence.

Does my dad's life amount to nothing more than a cautionary tale for me? That feels patently ridiculous. He had his own life, access to which is mine at best provisionally, partially, incompletely. I may be nothing but the wiseass, superior-sounding, full-of-himself punk who thinks he knows how to throw around uptown terms like "cautionary tale" with reference to my Brooklyn dad. He may have left the borough and the East Coast to save his own skin, but Brooklyn never left him. I could conceivably say the same about myself. And if there is any cautionary tale to be told, it might be this: *my* life constitutes the only cautionary tale I need for myself.

So what do I see in him? Was he a quester from Greenpoint, some smack-talking knight errant, viewed through the filter of my experience, my books, my memoirs? I could say yes and I could say no.

Did he determine the outlines of my life? Again, yes and no—and also maybe.

I have heard people say life is about making memories to treasure. But what if memory makes us who we are? Myth is a memory that never dies. Who am I then in the family myth, or the myth of myself?

～

MY DAD PLAYED THE horses every day possible, borrowing money when necessary, paying it back after booking a winner, or borrowing money elsewhere to pay it back when he booked a loser. Back in Brooklyn, he had borrowed from loan sharks, "shylocks," as he called them. A vicious cycle. He was addicted to what I presume to be the rush of the wager and the dream of the payoff, which I have to imagine sometimes, or rarely, got him back to square one, at which point the cycle played out again of borrowing and hoping to pay it all back if not being able to stiff creditors. He borrowed a few hundred from me a couple of times when I was fresh out of college, my first teaching job, pulling down a princely salary of $4,900 a year. He always paid it back, not that I was blasé about the risk I took. I am sympathetic. Well, now I am, when it is an abstract proposition. Back then, he induced a fear of impoverishment—his and my own.

At some point in California he started making much better money, and if he borrowed money ever again I have no idea. He gambled about every single day, and he lived his entire existence in California a mere few miles from Golden Gate Fields in Albany, to which he continually repaired. My mother railed against him without cease, to me, my brother, my wife, to anybody who was in the vicinity.

"The love of money is the root of all kinds of evil" (1 Timothy 6:10).

"The lack of money is the root of all evil" (Mark Twain).

I wrote my dissertation at Berkeley on Mark Twain, specifically the period of his career when he himself was tap city, the 1890s, publishing and barnstorming and striking business deals, chasing bad money with good, doing anything to keep the wolf from the door, taking one commercial risk after another. It didn't work, and then it worked, big time, because out of the ruins of his terrible business judgments, and his tragic family experience, he built the empire that was the public image of Mark Twain, great writer, great man, great American in his glorious white suit. This is a great country, which Samuel Langhorne Clemens, the first great anti-imperialist critic, took pains to excoriate.

❧

EVER SINCE ARISTOTLE'S *POETICS* we have cultivated a notion of the tragic figure. As we remember the definition, some star-crossed people, through some characterological failing or moral flaw, combined with the force of circumstances beyond their control, or via the handiwork of their personal demons, plummet to their inevitable doom. For the classical philosopher, the dramatization of this tragic flaw, if done masterfully, produces in the audience a catharsis. Catharsis is Aristotle's biological metaphor, referring to a kind of psychic, emotional purgation, analogized to other sorts of purgation, use your imagination. Catharsis for the audience is a welcome if wrenching release of pent-up emotion in response to the spectacle of the ruined tragic hero.

Nobody's life can be usefully examined, finally, as a work of art, though my father was more than once called *a piece of work*, with the attendant pejorative connotations. And everyone who watches the unfolding of another's life, from a close vantage point such as from within his family, hardly constitutes a theatrical audience. The theater is one or more removes away from family—though Oscar Wilde once called the Public an aggravated form of the family—and it takes a great artist to implicate a stranger in the drama of another. But it's more complicated than that. For there is a way for me to understand my old man as somebody with genuine flaws. He was a dark and tortured soul who felt powerless before his ingrained desires and designs—what he called his vice. But that, I think, trivializes the issue, and him. The vice stood for something, a desire for meaning, and the thrill of taking risk, and the hope for self-validation.

∽

I'M THE LAST ONE standing in my family.

There was a time when I would have claimed this was no big deal, that I'd felt like an outlier for as long as I could remember.

Now, I am not too sure. Death clears the decks.

For whom, besides myself, am I writing this book? *Who wantsta know?* as the old man would say.

Death clarifies. It's often observed we mourn someone we have lost, but also the loss of the connection we never had, the loss of the person we never knew. It's a commonplace observation, but there it is. There's nothing more commonplace than mortality. Mortality applies to the inevitably in everyone's life. My death is mine, however, and it's personal.

The things that might have happened—my mother happy, my father free of debt and money worry, my brother John content enough to survive in his own skin—never will happen because they never did happen. But to bring to mind the failed possibilities is important. Important to me, if nobody else, and perhaps to you, if you care for a minute or two.

I have a friend who is a building contractor, an excellent one. He's a complex, smart, hardworking, principled man. More than anything, he's a good man and, like many a good man, his life story is thorny: domestic turmoil, personal demons haunting him. He doesn't talk much about that sort of thing, but sometimes you can catch a glimpse of the pain behind his eyes, not that he's seeking your approval. He doesn't need my sympathy, but I admire him. I could call him stoic, but that sells him short. He has vulnerabilities and emotional depths, and those depths may contribute to the excellence of his work.

Once I asked him, as he was completing the punch list during the last days of his work for us, what drove him. Was it seeing the pleasure, the satisfaction in others who benefited from his skill and dedication? He did not hesitate. No, that wasn't it, not at all. It was all fine and good that his clients appreciated his work, but what pleased him was seeing for himself that he had done good work.

The question of the audience for a memoir, or any work of writing, is hard for me to answer. Who's the audience? You got me.

WHO'S GOING TO WIN the Super Bowl, the NBA championship, the World Series, the Stanley Cup, the Kentucky Derby?

Say you have an idea. Say you pick your team, your town, your horse. That's an opinion. This thought process of yours has absolutely nothing to do with taking the risk called making a wager. Yes, gambling on a game begins with a point of view, but that's only the beginning. You have to calculate the odds, analyze the situation, study the matchups and so on. Either that, or take a flyer.

You're still not close to gambling. Because when you finally put your money down, something takes place deep inside. It's akin to fear. And also anxiety. And exhilaration, too. Your self-worth is at stake along with your cash. Only idiots lose bets, right? Wrong. And I can prove it. When you bet and you lose, that doesn't tell your whole story. You hold a job, you enjoy some status in your world, you have people who love and need you. You don't have soup stains on your shirt or cigar ashes on your lap—that describes the idiots who bet the farm. You're simply losing. The waves of nausea overwhelm you. Are you a loser? How did you go from having an opinion about a game, or rooting for your hometown team to win, to feeling the humiliation of losing your money? No, you are not your money. It's more complicated. But you *are* your money when you make your play. And then after the final score, when you rip up your betting slip and limp away from the betting window, there's less of you than before.

∽

JESUS IS MANHANDLED AND scourged and brought up before the kangaroo court conducted by Pontius Pilate. Upon being questioned, Jesus says he has come into the world to testify to nothing less than the truth. "Everyone who belongs to the truth listens to my voice."

To which the son-of-a-bitch imperial functionary says: "What is truth?"

This might have been a good question had a better man asked it and asked it honestly—by which I mean unrhetorically. And though he finds no fault in Jesus, he does not let him go. Instead, insofar as it is the custom to free somebody on an occasion such as this, he asks the rabble what they want. In one voice, they cry out that they want a bandit named Barabbas to be exonerated and freed, and Pilate accedes, washing his hands. The world has not been the same since.

∽

FOR A WHILE, IN my forties, I was the associate head and academic dean of a Catholic high school. In fact, this was my alma mater, where I was once student body president and from which my brother had been expelled—to his great delight, I might add. It was not the best job I'd ever had, but the finest moments for me involved dealing with students who had committed acts of academic dishonesty, like plagiarism and cheating. As the culture of the school had devolved into a disaster, I had about one hundred cases land on my desk in my first year—this in a student body of fewer than four hundred.

This may sound surprising, but my conversations with kids in such straits were almost universally moving and deep, prying open, as they did, windows into their hearts, their minds, their souls, not to mention their families. The talks could go on for hours, and over multiple sessions. And there was never a dull moment. Ninety/ninety-five percent of the time, the results were positive. Most kids ultimately took responsibility, though usually not at first, and they began to understand what drove them. I haven't worked in a school for a long time now, and every school year with regularity appear articles and studies that purportedly show that cheating is suddenly an epidemic. I think it probably always has been and always will be. Until kids learn to reflect upon their own integrity—that is, until they're explicitly "invited" while undergoing some sort of crisis to reflect upon who they are—cheating is hard to resist.

Some kids walked into my office defiant, threatening legal action. Some kids, terrified, fearful some black mark was going to "go on their record." But no two cheaters—and no two teenagers—are the same. If you work with adolescents and fail to grasp that truth, you probably won't last long—they will eat you alive. If, that is, a vice principal like me doesn't scope that out and counsel you into another profession.

308 ~ JOSEPH DI PRISCO

Kids cheat for all sorts of reasons besides getting a better grade, though of course for some that seems to be the whole plan. Some kids cheat to please their parents, to live up to an idea their parents hold up for them, to increase their GPA in order to get into a "better college." Some kids cheat because teachers give them impossible assignments, or because they don't have the skills to manage the academic demands of the class. But since teenagers usually fake that they know more than they actually do, cheating feels like a natural opportunity.

The conversations eventually pivoted, if they did at all, when I saw my opening to say something like, "It's hard to be honest all the time." I am not suggesting there's a script I devised and followed, because there wasn't and I didn't. But in the moment, when an adult in my position owns up to the challenge of being honest, I found that a teenager gives himself permission to acknowledge he has made a mistake. "We all make mistakes. I made mistakes I have always regretted." I never told them this next part, but I cheated once in school, and didn't get caught, but I have never forgotten the whole sordid deal. I didn't tell them as much, because teenagers have practically zero tolerance for adult disclosures along those lines, when the old people were drunk or dishonest or stupid. A parent might get away with that once during high school, twice at the most, but it's mostly a non-starter, and here's why. Teenagers feel they are the exception to every rule. You might have learned from your mishaps, but it has nothing to do with your children; they are unique. Just ask them.

This goes to the next big moment. What the academic dean gets them to acknowledge is that, in their value scheme, there is almost nothing more important than being yourself. What follows from that is a question that blows up the conversation:

"So if being true to yourself is so important, then misrepresenting yourself in a paper or a test doesn't help you, does it?"

I'm probably being crudely schematic here, but teenagers know what the truth is, and it's valuable to them, too. I don't care what those surveys show.

As for parents, that's another story. Some families failed that test, they barged in blustery and threatening litigation or a punch in my nose (which did indeed happen), and as a consequence missed the opportunity to help their kids get through the ordeal. And they also missed the gift the school gave the whole family. Now that your child has cheated, and been caught, he has the opportunity to learn from that, and never do it again. It's hard to be honest all the time.

Of course, a few psychologically borderline kids didn't ever rise to the occasion, but many fewer than you'd expect. One sign of the proof: not very many of my students were repeat offenders. But there was one exception I remember.

Brian was a two-time offender. He was small of physical stature, even for a ninth grader, gentle of temper and clearly bright, and was popular enough not to qualify as an obvious candidate for being bullied. His dad was rock solid, too. He grasped what his son was going through, and he stood by the school, which was standing by his son. But now Brian was in significantly deeper trouble, having been caught again—I cannot remember the exact circumstances, but I believe it involved improperly sharing his work with another student on a test. He was an A student, by the way, and if you think A students don't cheat, you would be kidding yourself. As for Brian, consequences needed to be real for him, and they were about to ratchet up considerably now.

I think I might have given him a one-day in-school suspension for his first offense, to get his attention. And now I put him on notice: if there were a third violation, expulsion was the next option on the table. He thanked me for another chance, and said he would keep the bargain and never cheat again. He would tell his friends who were pressuring him for answers to tests that he was on a short leash. He believed that, given the stakes, they wouldn't put him in a bind again.

A week or so later, Brian knocked on my office door, downcast. He told me that he'd advised his friends what his situation was—and they were still pressuring him. He could not believe they were putting him in this spot. He was practically in tears when he realized, not that

I can recall his words, he was now on his own. He could come to me any time he wanted and we could talk, but I couldn't help him make his decisions in the moment he was being tested. He looked bereft, and I did my best to tell him that, finally, that's all there is, being on your own when it came to becoming an honest man. It isn't easy being honest, ever.

As far as I am aware, Brian never got in school trouble again, and I have every reason to hope he has been living a good and full life, yet I think about him—and I can visualize his crestfallen face—and hope that he was not permanently disillusioned. Then again, what did I know? Well, if I knew anything in the world, I did know it was hard to be honest all the time.

～

MY BEST FRIEND SINCE the seventh grade, someone behind whom I sat at my desk in our Catholic school in Berkeley, and who later became my son's godfather, tells a story. When his son was six or seven, the boy was mixing it up with a chum, boisterously talking trash in the backyard. From inside the house, Bernie eavesdropped on them going at it. They were doing the my-dad-is-better-than-your-dad dozens. My dad is stronger than your dad, my dad can run faster than your dad, my dad can hit a baseball farther than your dad—that sort of thing. Finally, Bernie's son had had enough:

"Yeah, well, my dad has a bigger penis."

And Bernie said to himself, "You tell him, Joel."

❧

DID I SECRETLY WISH my father had been not some small-time hood, but a John Gotti? I could answer that either way and be telling the truth.

Would I really have wished him to be somebody out of *Goodfellas*? Really?

I think of my oldest grandson, first born of my only son. If you were in my vicinity, I could be showing you photogenic snaps of him and his two siblings on my phone, so consider yourself off the hook. Once, we were waiting for a movie to begin, rainy day, he was seven or eight, and we wandered into a nearby bookstore in the mall till showtime came around. He's a very bookish boy, the kind who used to carry *Diary of a Wimpy Kid* to the playground, so that was a congenial destination for him. As it happened, a book of mine was then being featured in the new books section. By reflex, I took it down to have a look, can't quite explain. He noticed what I was doing and had a question:

"You really like yourself, don't you?" Then we both cracked up, he got me.

Another time, he wanted to know:

"Nonno, are you famous?"

I tell him no, not at all.

But he isn't satisfied, I can tell, and he badly wants to believe otherwise.

At some later point I was walking him and his friend home from school—perhaps when he was nine. His pal wanted to know who was the old guy trailing, keeping them company.

"That's my nonno, he's a famous author."

He likes to take down books from my shelves. Once without warning he spent a few hours reading my novel *All for Now*, though what he was taking in was hard for me to determine. I hoped he wasn't understanding it, given the unremittingly R-rated jokes and the fundamentally tragic story. I didn't want to snatch the book from his hands, because that would supercharge his curiosity and mystify the subject and the author. His wise, loving parents do their best to guide him in his reading. As he put it, "They don't want me to read about things I don't understand. They mean like sex. But I read stuff all the time I don't understand." (I'm looking forward to his adolescence.) In any case, that day, when he was ready, he and I tried to discuss what he took from the book of mine, didn't get very far, which was comforting. Whew, close call. I told his father about the incident, and all Mario could say was it was just like his boy, but then he added: "Let's keep him away from *Subway to California* for a long time."

Once when he met some new kids, my son reported that as they were getting to know each other, what video games and music they liked, and so on, the boy asked the others, by way of an icebreaker, I suppose: "So, have you read *All for Now*?"

Do we all want the major figures in our lives to be larger than life? Yes, I suppose we might. Did I give over to that fantasy myself with my father? I think I probably did. Which is on one level crazy, and on another, normal.

✑

FATHERS AND SONS, BONDED by their lies to each other. Separated by their truthfulness. Never ask a question you don't know or want the answer to. Words for attorneys to live by, as well as by fathers and their sons. Also Russian novelists and Shakespeare. But I digress.

I began by searching out the predicate for our flight from Brooklyn to California. That led me into performing a type of exhumation of my past and my family's.

Yes, it was traumatic for a ten-year-old boy like me to be abruptly, inexplicably uprooted from home and friends and dropped down—infinitely dropped, as Winnicott put it—in a state of incredible, awful beauty Didion would have her way with because it required that correction. And it was all about the lifesaving lies and necessary deceptions of my father. Lies told to preserve himself and his freedom.

And the trade-off for me was that eventually it proved mostly to my benefit, being liberated from Brooklyn to the fantastic city of Berkeley, with California being a land of inestimable opportunity. And sunshine. And no snow. Who knows what sort of life I might have led had I stayed? Not that such speculation is ultimately interesting to me.

∾

As a child I was continually anxious and fearful, always on guard, listening for approaching footsteps, on the lookout for somebody coming up behind me, not necessarily figuratively, either. My condition ought not to be confused with PTSD. That would be overstatement. When I was eight or nine I took to carrying around for protection not a switchblade (as my older brother did) but a pocket knife, without a clear concept about what I would do with such an impractical weapon.

My compulsive behaviors, as early as when I was five or six, encouraged my mother to take me to the doctor. I was continually washing my hands. She recounted the story to me and others a hundred times and highlighted my beloved pediatrician's diagnosis and prescription: no big deal, and I should slather lotion on my dried-out paws. Her account cut both ways. She wanted to prove that she was a good mother and I was a drama queen.

It took a long time to get some measure of control over the hand washing and my generalized compulsivity and anxiety. I must have employed a type of cognitive behavior therapy upon myself, not that I knew the term. Not surprisingly, when I was a young adult I found myself inside the offices of one psychotherapist after another.

Perhaps my favorite was one I found in California. He was a native New Yorker, and an eminent figure on the national psychological scene. He wrote a haunting, graphic book that tackled nothing less than the nature of evil, and he espoused the benefits of hypnosis, and he was hilarious and kind, and not too easy on me. I was never hypnotized (as far as I was aware) but he helped me face myself, including my debilitating obsessive checking and rechecking. It was deceptively simple, what he did.

What if, for instance, I left the keys in my car, he wanted to know, what would be the worst that could happen? We talked at length through this horrifying, to me, hypothetical. We grasped it was about the maintenance of a sense of order and control, since order and control were hardly ever givens in my mind. We could have chosen other equally dreadful hypotheticals that obsessed me, like leaving a door unlocked, like losing a button on my shirt, like parking the car outside the lines, like turning in a paper with a misspelled word.

I believe I know that the back door is definitely locked, but I don't *know* the door is definitely locked, or know the door is definitely locked, or KNOW it, for that matter. Besides, what harm could it do, to check, to put my mind at rest? Mind at rest? That's the plan? Good luck. Do you always talk to yourself when you're checking? Yes, you got a problem with that?

And check a few more times.

And then a few more times more.

This whole exhausting project must sound loony tunes to a non-compulsive person. Good for you, non-compulsive person, you're lucky. You probably also get to appointments on time, too.

Psychiatrists might have recently landed on a beta-blocker, propranolol, that, when combined with exposure therapy, seems to work wonders addressing or curing incapacitating anxieties. I myself am not pathological, therefore not a worthy candidate for the protocol. Because that day as my shrink and I talked through what it would mean to leave my keys or lose my keys, we—I mean I— reached this conclusion: the worst that could happen, whatever it was, was something I could survive. I wouldn't perish, I wouldn't crack up. I cannot explain how liberating this was to me. As I write these sentences now I cannot believe how such a simple idea flooded me with hopefulness. There was hope. Sometimes hope is enough.

But let's go back. Did my childhood obsessive behaviors (which have persisted well into my adult life) connect to whatever level of trauma I experienced in my early home life? I could not say with any degree of certitude, but I never for a minute viewed myself as a victim. I construed my life as conforming to a type of norm, the way all children strive to do, no matter how apparently dysfunctional the family system would seem to an outsider. Yes, my family was normal and that was Brooklyn, notions that locked together like

Legos. I never felt physically threatened in or by my home life, if, that is, I discount the high level of rage my parents expressed toward each other—which I probably shouldn't do. Having an unreliable mother probably affected my conceptions of love and undermined my psychic security, but she's not to blame for my poor romantic track record in the past. Having a mostly absentee father surely unsteadied my existential underpinnings, as did the anxiety he himself had to have felt, and unconsciously or consciously transmitted, while being under constant pressure as he gambled compulsively and lived his life of petty crime. The effects had to have been anything but negligible for him—and for me and my brother. And then the flight out of Brooklyn, taking that subway to California: that disturbed and angered me. It must have eroded any residual sense I had of order and control. Those tumultuous feelings I mostly repressed—repressed and then probably sublimated into schoolwork and my faith. I would also write poems, which I started doing around ten or eleven, and borrow stacks of library books, and seek out those brighter, warmer, organized, alternative worlds where I could take up residence. I may have been solitary but I felt welcomed by the disembodied presences located on the page. I was keeping company with all the figures of my imagination and I could bring them to life in my head and sometimes on the page.

～

SOMETIMES I'M ASKED WHEN I "decided" to become a writer. It's not something I know how to address. For one thing, I'm not so sure *decision* is the right term. I was always entranced by the idea of being a writer. *Old Yeller, The Good Earth, Of Mice and Men*, the stories of Flannery O'Connor and O. Henry, the poems of Stephen Crane and Percy Bysshe Shelley and William Carlos Williams—these works moved me as a boy, they made me wish to make such things on my own. Very early on, I remember reading what one writer said—cannot recall who, but it could have been any of a hundred—something to the effect, Don't try to become a writer unless you cannot picture not being one. This ensnared my attention. But the admonition didn't intimidate me at perhaps thirteen years old—definitely not the way pretty girls effortlessly did. Instead, the opposite: it emboldened me. Of course, I thought, of course, that's right, and that's me. It was related to a notion that transfixed me around the same time. I vividly recall my brilliant ninth grade English teacher (and he truly was, and by all accounts still is, brilliant) using in class a phrase exotic to me: *vicarious experience.* I struggled to wrap my mind around the idea of experiencing somebody else's experience. After all, I was busy trying to have an experience or two of my own, even if it didn't involve any of those pretty girls. And then it gradually clarified for me. *Bingo*, vicarious experience was literature's best trick. And that was the thing, I would learn and relearn over and over, that keyed the pleasure, the work, the challenge of both the reader's and the writer's imagination. At thirteen I showed my teacher the stories I wrote before I sent them to magazines. He didn't discourage or flatter me, either, but *Esquire* didn't bite.

All this brings up another question for somebody like me much later in life, perhaps predictably. Are writers gamblers at heart? Is it strange to think there might be resemblances between the two? Both risk precious assets. In one case, time and intellectual energy and earning capacity; in the other, time, intellectual energy, and cash money. Serious exposure, then, for both. Both may yearn for the big payout. Is the payout for an author obvious? Riches, fame, awards? It may be true what Samuel Johnson said, that "no man but a blockhead ever wrote, except for money," and who would be fool enough to take on Dr. Johnson? He's inarguably correct to this extent: a writer without audience is often in dire straits, emotionally or psychologically and usually financially. Not to say that pleasing the public is ever the unalloyed objective of a good writer, nor does the measure of interest in a writer define achievement or success or satisfaction however defined—sales, likes, viral tweets, movie deals, book prizes, and so on. Well, that's the story of me, and I'm sticking to it.

Literary history is the chronicle of great writers disregarded or demeaned by their contemporaries; the tale of writers who created the audience for their work before the public was ready. But not so fast, buddy boy. For every obscure Joyce, there's a rabidly popular Shakespeare; for every moody arcane dead-lettering Melville, there's a show-stopping celebrity Dickens. Yet it was T. S. Eliot who said that, for the purposes of cultural advancement, a good poet is as valuable as a great poet, and may be more important. I never cared much for the world-famous Gentleman from Saint Louis's cult of impersonality or his poetry (except for "Prufrock"), and his essays have not worn well over time. But as for most writers, why pony up to the betting window in the first place? I can only speak for myself.

For me, I'm not sure where to find the writer's betting window. Unless it's inside myself. I'll never find out immediately after the working writer's equivalent of a football game, a race, a hand of cards, what I have earned. I do my work, and that is its own reward, if there is one. If somebody reads it and finds momentary delight, that's a bonus, more than enough for me. If I lose a bet on the Warriors, say, I have lost my money, true. If I lose a bet on a book, if, that is, the reviewers ignore it or dismiss it, if readers stay away in droves, what have I lost? Snark monsters wield sharp knives. Honestly, it can be depressing recognition, even if I can expertly fake insouciance, and even if the bottle of Irish beckons with its midday Siren's call. But one goes on. At least I *have* gone on, so far. That inclination may link to my lifelong disposition, coming straight out of my Brooklyn with a father like mine; it may indeed be that I am congenitally undiscourageable. Resilient or stubborn? Survivor or deluded fool? Or maybe too dense to absorb the message from the universe? Then again, my suspicion is that, ever since the Big Bang, the "universe" is probably too preoccupied to bother imparting a message to anyone, least of all me.

As my old man put it so memorably to me as a young writer, poetry won't pay the light bill. But if I am lucky, as I have been once or twice, I might confiscate some electricity, enough to illuminate my way for a while anyway.

In this context, there's one more thing I might say about my dad and mom and it's something that, at this late date, surprises me to acknowledge. They were indeed incredibly difficult people, essentially unmanageable and maddening and unfathomably irrational. But some days I do miss them. Particularly my father. I feel sad for him, for the life he led and for the life he didn't or the life he never conceived, to the extent that maybe this whole book in your hands is an elegy to him—and maybe also to my childhood and my brother's. If I could explain these feelings to my satisfaction, hundred to one I would have never written a single word.

New York State Appellate Division

RECORDS AND BRIEFS

POLICE DEPARTMENT CITY OF NEW YORK

Case #33613

April 23, 1962.

IN THE MATTER of Charges Against PATROLMAN PETER R. CELENTANO, #837237, Shield #4477, 30th Precinct, of the Police Force, Police Department, City of New York.

Upon reading and filing cfertain written charges in this matter, wherein he is charged with Violation Of The Rules And Procedures, dated April 18th, 1961, duly made and preferred in the form and manner prescribed by law and the rules and procedures of the said Police Department by Captain Sydney C. Cooper, P.C.C.I.U., against the said Patrolman Peter R. Celentano, a member of the police force of said city, and it having been duly proved that a copy of such charges, together with a written notice that the same had been made and preferred against him, the said Patrolman Peter R. Celentano, requiring him to appear and answer thereto at a proper time and place named in said notice, has been duly served upon him, the said Patrolman Peter R. Celentano, in the manner required by law and the said rules and procedures; and he, the said Patrolman Peter R. Celentano, having appeared and answered at the time and place mentioned and required by said notice, and the said charges having been duly brought to a hearing, and duly tried, heard, publicly examined and investigated, in the manner required by law and the rules and procedures of the said Police Department before Hon. Louis L. Roos, Assistant to the Police Commissioner, on the 15th and 25th days of May, 1961, and before Hon. Leonard E. Reisman, Deputy Police Commissioner, on the 21st and 29th days of June, the 15th day of August, the 20th day of October, and the 2nd, 6th, and 14th days of November, and the 6th day of December, 1961, and a full opportunity having been afforded to the said Patrolman Peter R. Celentano, to be heard in his defense, and the proofs and allegations in relation to said charges having been duly taken and recorded as required by law and the said rules and procedures, and the determination of said charges, based upon the entire record adduced at the hearing, and the findings and recommendations made thereon, having been referred to the Police Commissioner, the Police Commissioner, upon due consideration and review of said findings and recommendations, and upon inquiry of and consultation with said Trial Commissioner, adjudges the said Patrolman Peter R. Celentano, to be Guilty, of the Charges, and Guilty, of specification 1, Not Guilty, of specifications 2, and 3, and does convict him of the Charges, and of specification 1, and upon such conviction, adjudges and determines that he, the said Patrolman Peter R. Celentano, be, and he hereby is, Dismissed from the Police Force, Police Department, City of New York. MICHAEL J. MURPHY Police Commissioner

Joe and Caza Di Prisco. Berkeley, California circa 1967.

Pope's mother and father and his two sons (and his German Shepherd).

KEEPING WATCH

My brother Eddie died of liver failure at NYU hospital in February 2002. He was fifty-nine.

My brother John died of a heroin overdose on his bathroom floor in San Francisco in January 2003. He was fifty-one.

My brother Bobby died of lung cancer in a Coney Island hospital in the middle of night, March 2008. He was sixty-four.

My mother died of congestive heart failure and Alzheimer's in Florida in January 2010, one day after her birthday. She was eighty-six.

My father died in Northern California in July 2012, like his wife also of congestive heart failure and Alzheimer's, at his assisted living residence. He was eighty-seven.

They are all buried alongside each other in a Catholic cemetery, overlooking Brooklyn.

∽

Looking back over that cruel catalogue, I have a complicated reaction. On the one hand, life seems increasingly ephemeral. But on the other, I feel the opposite, too: that these lives my family lived will always matter, to me, of course, but to many others as well I could name—and in fact, people I have named in this book and in my previous memoir. So anything but fleeting, because look: there they are, memorialized on the page. Memorialized inadequately, to be sure, by me, using whatever limited resources of information and imagination I have at my disposal.

There are few extant narratives of their lives, fashioned by themselves, except for some letters, those trial transcripts, and my recollections of their words and deeds. If I shunt them into narratives of my own devising, because they for the most part left no written record, I stand vulnerable to the charge of misappropriation, for my own self-serving purposes. I might also be accused of expropriation, though given they are all gone, I wonder if that is logically feasible. In any case, my motivations may indeed be suspect. You may believe I am selling myself as an example of redemption, and this book is nothing more than self-promotion. To that criticism I would respond: I have never felt redeemed, not for a minute.

I remember them. Is that enough? No, not for me. I can hear the way they laughed, I can see the way they walked into a room, I can taste the food they cooked. I cannot legitimately suggest at every juncture that I am narrating pieces of their lives. All I can say is that these are my accounts of how I remembered them and what they meant to me. I don't think I have treated them unfairly, though I may not be in the best position to know; that might be the task of my reader, if not my confessor or confidant. My complex relationships with each of them were sometimes painful, sometimes joyous, but they remain unforgettable.

As for that catalogue of the dead above, I also envision the one name missing, so far. I glimpse the gaping opening for one more, my own.

ONE TIME MY THREE brothers and I went out together, a night on the town. Early seventies, I believe. I could say we were partying, but it's impossible to remember the plan or who formed it. I remember sitting on the subway taking the GG from Brooklyn to Queens, then the L to Manhattan, heading to a club of some kind. I wonder whose idea the excursion was, or the purpose, beyond being together. It must have been a fall or spring night, because winter coats are not in evidence in my memory, but I recall I was in college at the time, an alien place none of them would experience firsthand. The recollection is so crisp, so luminous, and at the same time so blurred, like so many recollections of me with them. I do know for a fact that I was happy to be there with my brothers. I don't know how the evening went or how it ended, but I was conscious in the moment that the occasion would never be repeated—and it wasn't.

～

MONSIGNOR SHANE HAS BEEN there for so many big events in the life of my family and me. Another way to put it: he has been there in the sacred moments, which is the functional definition of a sacrament. He's celebrated Mass for us and consecrated the Eucharist. He baptized and confirmed Mario and served as his spiritual mentor, too, when he was a boy who converted, of his own volition, to Catholicism. Shane also presided at the wedding of Patti and me. He visited John in prison, which doesn't qualify as a sacrament, exactly, but maybe it ought to. He administered last rites to my dad. By my count, that amounts to at least five of the seven Catholic sacraments. I could also probably add a sixth sacrament of Reconciliation, what used to be called Confession, because he has heard me out in my darkest hours. I was talking with him recently and reminded him. He laughed when he said, "True, but I never gave you absolution." Then again, I never asked. Sometimes, you can't get forgiveness from someone else.

What about my father's religious inclinations—he who was tagged Pope for having been supposedly outed when he was caught strolling out of a church? And let's stipulate that he did indeed make a visit. Did he light a candle, did he make his own confession, did he fall on bended knee and pray? I will never know what if anything he was seeking there.

A handful of times in his seventies he asked us to take him to Mass, but he might have merely wanted to hang with his grandson on a Sunday morning. He never addressed the subject of belief, or disbelief for that matter, around me. In this context, I have to note that there was a seventeenth-century French genius of probability theory who is famous for a certain formulation. Pascal argued it was on balance better to subscribe to God's existence, because the risk of eternal damnation outweighs any possible benefits of concluding otherwise. As he put it: "If you win you win everything, if you lose you lose nothing." For most of his life, my dad rarely passed up a chance to make a bet. Considering the infinite upside of this speculative opportunity, he certainly made worse bets than Pascal's Wager. Why wouldn't he bank on the possibility—*Baby needs a new pair of shoes*— he just might hit the ultimate jackpot?

∽

AS HIS DAYS BEGAN to dwindle down I took him to the track whenever he asked, memorable moments for me if not him, because the Alzheimer's was already eroding his brain. For one such excursion, we went to Golden Gate Fields in Albany, California, and he put his money down on a horse to win the 2010 Kentucky Derby. The horse went off nine to one. "Sounds right," he said before he bet it, spitting on the favorite, who would ultimately finish out of the money. Unlike millions of other gamblers, and despite his cognitive deficits, he bet the winner, a horse named Super Saver. Great call on the part of this handicapper, but there was no saving him from Alzheimer's.

⁓

AFTER HE SETTLED INTO his assisted living residence, he seemed to enjoy coming over for supper to our house, a thirty-minute drive away. We picked him up or arranged for a ride in a car service he had championed long ago, chauffeured by an Indian woman who treated him gently and respectfully. He always wanted the same dish for Sunday supper: Patti's spaghetti Bolognese. She is a great cook, and he ate with deliberate gusto and in monkish silence, as was his custom, before his appetite permanently wandered off. And it soon became progressively more challenging for him to be away, even for brief spells, from his residence. A proud man, he was occasionally bushwhacked by the betrayals of his own bodily functions.

Otherwise, we regularly visited my dad as his final descent began, virtually daily. Sometimes he was shuttled outside in a wheelchair into the lovely gardens to spend some time with a hospice dog. These outings became increasingly rare for him. It could be tough to sit up in a wheelchair. When he stayed indoors and we entered his apartment, he would usually be lodged in his easy chair, staring into the middle distance in the quiet and curtained shadows, which he preferred. When he noticed us, he invariably greeted us the same way each time:

"Oh, shit."

This made us always laugh; how else could we respond? Was *Oh, shit* an exclamation of surprise, a complaint, a smack? I don't know. It was the signature exclamation of my old man from Brooklyn.

He and I battled before dementia and we battled after, when it wasn't a fair fight. I confiscated car keys; he was a danger on the road. He was always demanding more razor blades (he had a stock pile) or more toothpaste (the cabinet overflowed). Personal hygiene was always a major consideration for this fastidious man, even toward the end. The TV remote vanquished him. I commandeered credit cards, paid his bills. He loathed that I had financial control, though conceded: "Guess you're an honest guy." High praise from a man like him.

He didn't speak at length or coherently, and when he talked at all he seemed to be struggling to get his bearings. One fairly recurrent question emerged:

"Have you talked to my wife lately?"

And that's the way he phrased it, not have I talked to my *mother*. Once or twice in the past, I had tried to tell him that his wife was not here anymore, which I know now was something I shouldn't have done. That was when he looked at me like I was an idiot, or that I was pulling one over on him. It had been a couple of years since she had died, but what did that matter to him?

We would pass the hours together, our conversation, such as it was, disjointed, haphazard, minimalist. After a while, I ceased responding to the literal content of his statements and queries, and I listened, even to the silence, tried to be present, till that, too, became excruciating—for me and perhaps for him.

He had round-the-clock care on the part of a team of Tongan helpers, a concierge doctor, at some point hospice nurses, as well as other nurses and caremangers at the residence, along with his loyal care manager. And also my wife, Patti, who was a trooper and who faithfully showed up, often bringing fresh changes of clothes. She and my dad genuinely liked each other.

We sensed one day that the death watch had, almost without our awareness, already sneaked upon us. And we also sensed that, no matter how many of us were looking after him, we were outnumbered by the singular specter of dying.

I was leveled one day by a new question, one I had never anticipated and one that he would never repeat.

"Is John coming by?"

It had been almost ten years since my father and I embraced by the side of my brother's casket. But yes, that was indeed a crucial question a dying father like him, and a brother like me, would wish to have answered.

∽

So what is, finally, the truth about my family and me? How do I make sense of his life and how I grew up and who I became?

My father's experience contributed to the making of who I am, for better or worse. I see traces of him everywhere—in my own domestic life, and in my own work. I think I understand better now what I dimly grasped as a little boy: that my journey from Brooklyn made me feel like I didn't belong anywhere, certainly not California. But maybe that is one key to being a writer, at least one like me. My father had this in common with me: we always conceived of ourselves as outsiders.

These family traces can appear to be indistinguishable from scars, but scars can be eloquent if not always beautiful. At least they have their own stories to tell. My sometimes turbulent early home life necessitated the development of my own self-reliance, even as it richly colored my experience—and made the world seem risky and dramatic. Resisting my mother and father's suspect values helped me create my own, or discover others that were more useful or profound for me. My internal life deepened. I found myself drawn, intellectually and emotionally, to the realms of literature and art. That didn't mean that the darker realms didn't hold their appeal at various times, and that demons similar to my dad's wouldn't have their way. Could I have spoken of such matters to my parents? I suppose I could have, although I cannot say I did, and I doubt my ideas would have made much sense to them. Does that matter? To me, it does, which is why my family reminiscences, including the happier ones, are tinged with regret and disappointment. I don't blame them, let's be clear, for their choices. They were who they were. And without them, I wouldn't be me. Again, for better or worse.

As for my father, he will always be my dad.

My dad compulsively betting the horses.

My dad in the wind.

My dad testifying in trials.

My dad under indictment.

My dad who dragged us, without a plan beyond his immediate survival, to California.

My dad who had moments of pride and moments of incomprehension. My dad who couldn't fathom the bottomless pain he felt when John was an addict and died alone on a bathroom floor. My dad who was the adoring, faithful grandfather of my son. My dad who was dominated by his gambling "vice," and swallowed up by his insanely loyal relationship to my mother, his wife. Also my dad who in his thwarted way loved his boys and couldn't do much about how they grew up.

Complicated man, Joe Di Prisco. All things considered, that's maybe not the bleakest epitaph in the world.

His death is simply one final stage of our never-ending relationship, and there's no *simply* about that. I will always be Popey's son. And yet he remains a question mark. Maybe I did not know him while I was growing up, but then in the end we came full circle: as he was dying he couldn't recognize me at all.

My whole life I tried to read him. I came to see how I had to write him for myself. I guess he was correct from the beginning when I badgered him with my childhood questions. I *was* always writing this book, my book about the Pope of Brooklyn. That was true at the time, and it still is.

RECORDS & SOURCES

CRIMINAL DETAILS AND LEGAL matters cited, including trial testimony contained in transcripts published in *New York State Appellate Division Records and Briefs*, in addition to case files that were unsealed:

New York Supreme Court
Appellate Division—First Department
In the Matter of Peter R. Celentano
Index #12162/1962
October 25, 1962

New York Supreme Court
Appellate Division—First Department
In the Matter of Baldasaro P. Ficalora
Index #15830/1963
November 18, 1963

New York Supreme Court

Appellate Division—First Department

In the Matter of John Tatarian

Index #14525/1963

November 15, 1963

New York Supreme Court

Appellate Division—First Department

In the Matter of John Tatarian

June 11, 1964

Supreme Court: Queens County

Criminal Term Part III

The People of the State of New York

Against Joseph Di Prisco, Defendant

Indictment No. 1120-61

December 11, 1962

Files unsealed November 25, 2015

Brooklyn: King's County

Indictment number 543-62, filed in 1962

Records destroyed in a warehouse fire

U.S. Department of Justice

Federal Bureau of Investigation

Subject: Joseph Di Prisco et al

Freedom of Information Act request; December 10, 2010

FBI San Francisco File 156B-SF-92738

Poetics, Aristotle

The Color of Money, directed by Martin Scorsese; screenplay by
    Richard Price (1986)

Confessions, Saint Augustine

The City of God, Saint Augustine

Letters and Papers from Prison, Dietrich Bonhoeffer

Cheesebox: Being the Life and Times of Cheesebox Callahan, Paul S.
    Meskil and Gerard Callahan

Unauthorized Freud, Frederick Crews, editor

Slouching Towards Bethlehem, Joan Didion

Among the Dangs, George P. Elliott

The Great Gatsby, F. Scott Fitzgerald

"Why I'm Over Confessional Writing," Emily Fox Gordon;
    The American Scholar, Spring 2015

Catch-22, Joseph Heller

The Gospel According to John

The Divided Self, R. D. Laing

The Man Who Outgrew His Prison Cell: Confessions of a Bank Robber, Joe Loya

A Good Man is Hard to Find, Flannery O'Connor

The Complete Essays of Montaigne, translated by Donald M. Frame

The Better Angels of our Nature: Why Violence Has Declined, Steven Pinker

Far from the Tree: Parents, Children, and the Search for Identity, Andrew Solomon

The Noonday Demon: An Atlas of Depression, Andrew Solomon

Serpico, directed by Sidney Lumet (1973)

The Wizard of Oz, directed by Victor Fleming, et al; based on novels by Frank L. Baum (1939)

Saint Augustine, Garry Wills

Playing and Reality, D. W. Winnicott

The Child and the Outside World, D. W. Winnicott

On the Child, D. W. Winnicott

Bender, New and Selected Poems by Dean Young

Subway to California, Joseph Di Prisco

Acknowledgments

The author wishes to thank:

Mario Di Prisco and Family

Regan McMahon

Monsignor Shane

Katherine Palermo

Jennifer Palermo Bobe

Katharine Michaels

Elizabeth Trupin-Pulli, JET Literary Associates

Tyson Cornell, Publisher, Rare Bird

Julia Callahan, Hailie Johnson, and Guy Intoci of Rare Bird

Not-Naomi, Esquire, and research staff

Robert Gearty, intrepid and invaluable researcher

Kathleen Caldwell and A Great Good Place for Books,
*   Oakland, California*

Kim Dower (aka Kim-from-LA)

Francesca Applegarth. Nina Rothberg Bailey. Jim and Lela Barnes. Tracey Borst and Robert Menicucci. Jennie Chabon. Peter Chastain. Brent Cohen. Laura Cogan. Josephine Courant. Diane Del Signore. Anthony and Nan Fredotovich. Jane and Jeff Green. Bernard and Cheryl Hooper. Blair Jackson. Kathy and Tony Laglia. Ralph and Liz Long. Amber Lowi. Christine McQuade. Donald McQuade. Jim and Katherine Moule. Beth Needel. David Robins. Anne Rosenthal. Peter Sackman. Vickie Sciacca. Robyn Simonett. A. R. Taylor. Robert Tembeckjian. Carlton Tucker. Oscar Villalon. Dan Wilcox. Laurie Saurborn and Dean Young.

Patti James and Family

BOROUGH OF **Manhattan**

* All records of indict-
ments pending against
Joseph Di Prisco.
ARRESTED 9/28/61

HE PEOPLE OF THE STATE OF NEW YORK:

To **County Court, County of Queens**

REETINGS:

* **produce**

WE COMMAND YOU, that all business and excuses being laid aside, you appear and ~~attend~~ before the Police Commisioner

the Police Department, City of New York, at the Trial Room of that Department No. **240 Centre** street, Borough

Manhattan in the City of New York, **8** day of **February** 19 **62**, at **10:30** o'clock **A. M.**,

testify and give evidence concerning the matters alleged in a certain charge or charges now pending AGAINST

Ptl. Tatarian - L.D.S. then and there to be publicly examined into.

AND IF YOU FAIL so to do you will be liable, in addition to any other punishment which may be lawfully inflicted

erefor, for the damages sustained by the person aggrieved, in consequence of the failure and fifty dollars in addition thereto.

WITNESS: **Michael J. Murphy** Police Commissioner, of the Police Department, City of New York,

the office of the said Police Commissioner in the City of New York, the **5** day of **February** 19**62** .

Michael J. Murphy
(Police Commissioner)

23

COUNTY COURT: QUEENS COUNTY

THE PEOPLE OF THE STATE OF NEW YORK

against ·

JOSEPH DI PRISCO.

Defendant.s

THIRD COUNT

THE GRAND JURY OF THE COUNTY OF QUEENS, by this indictment, accuse the

defendant **s** of the crime of **GRAND** LARCENY **IN THE SECOND DEGREE**

committed as follows:

The defendant **s, aforenamed, acting in concert, and aiding and being**

aided by an accomplice who is known to the Grand Jury

on or about **February 11th, 1961**

in the County of Queens

stole and took from the possession of **STEVEN SIPOS**

the following property of the value of **$105.75**

namely: **United States currency in that amount**

owned by **STEVEN SIPOS**

with the intent to deprive the owner thereof, and of the use and benefit thereof, and to appropriate the same

to the use of the defendant. **s and their said accomplice.**